D080096?

Positive Discipline for Your Stepfamily

Also in the
POSITIVE DISCIPLINE Series

Positive Discipline for Your Stepfamily

Nurturing Harmony, Respect, and Joy in Your New Family

Jane Nelsen, Ed.D.

Cheryl Erwin, M.A.

H. Stephen Glenn, Ph.D.

PRIMA PUBLISHING
3000 Lava Ridge Court • Roseville, California 95661
(800) 632-8676 • www.primalifestyles.com

© 2000 by Jane Nelsen, Cheryl Erwin, and H. Stephen Glenn

All rights reserved. No part of this book may be reproduced or transmitted in any form or by any means, electronic or mechanical, including photocopying, recording, or by any information storage or retrieval system, without written permission from Prima Publishing, except for the inclusion of brief quotations in review.

All products mentioned in this book are trademarks of their respective companies.

PRIMA PUBLISHING and colophon are trademarks of Prima Communications Inc., registered with the United States Patent and Trademark Office.

Illustrations by Paula Gray

Library of Congress Cataloging-in-Publication Data

Nelsen, Jane.
  Positive discipline for your stepfamily : nurturing harmony, respect, and joy in your new family / Jane Nelsen, Cheryl Erwin, H. Stephen Glenn.
    p. cm. — (Positive discipline series)
  ISBN 0-7615-2012-0
  1. Stepfamilies. 2. Stepchildren. 3. Discipline of children. I. Glenn, H. Stephen. II. Erwin, Cheryl. III. Title. IV. Series.

HQ759392 .N47 2000
306.874—dc21   00-058889
                                                       CIP

00 01 02 03 DD 10 9 8 7 6 5 4 3 2 1
Printed in the United States of America

HOW TO ORDER

Single copies may be ordered from Prima Publishing, 3000 Lava Ridge Court, Roseville CA 95661; telephone (800) 632-8676, ext. 4444. Quantity discounts are also available. On your letterhead, include information concerning the intended use of the books and the number of books you wish to purchase.

Visit us online at www.primalifestyles.com

CONTENTS

INTRODUCTION

W E A L L K N O W H E R. In fact, most of us grew up hearing fairy tales about her: the wicked stepmother who stole a loving father's affection and forced his poor children to sleep in a coal bin, wear rags, and scrub floors while her children (usually rude, unattractive young people) lived like princes and princesses. Since she and her male counterpart, the cruel stepfather, were almost always ugly, nasty, and thoroughly despicable, we celebrated when they finally got what was coming to them.

Like most figures in fairy tales, the wicked stepmother is a wild exaggeration woven around a kernel of truth. Remarrying, combining families, and learning to live with and parent children not your own are huge challenges. It is a rare stepparent who can navigate these treacherous waters without an occasional shipwreck. Our cultural stereotypes and expectations are not much help, either; stepparents have had a bad reputation throughout the ages. Is it any wonder, then, that so many adults face remarrying and blending their families with fear and trepidation?

The simple truth is that beginning a new relationship, living together, and combining separate families into one are complex jobs with many pitfalls. For instance, it's difficult to know how to describe this new sort of family— or what to call the people in it. Everyone is familiar with the term "stepfamily," but people often want to avoid the old, familiar stereotypes, so they have invented all sorts of new variations. Stepfamilies are sometimes called "remarried families" or "reconstituted families" (sounds a bit like orange juice, doesn't it?). Or they are called "blended families," which does a good job of describing what happens, although it does make people sound a little like stew ingredients.

In this book we will use the term "stepfamily" to describe families in which either or both adults bring one or more children from a previous relationship and decide to live together and, perhaps, to add children of their own. We will talk about "stepparents" because there doesn't seem to be another word for that role. Whichever terms we use, we mean them with great respect for the people who have chosen to try again and to tackle an especially challenging job.

It is the goal of this book—and the hope of its authors—that those who contemplate forming a stepfamily (and those already part of one) will discover ways to identify potential pitfalls and gain skills to avoid them. We hope that you will find real solutions to real problems and reassurance that the adjustment to stepfamily living rarely comes without difficult moments—and that those difficult moments do not mean your stepfamily can never be a healthy and encouraging place to live. In a recent article, Kay Morgan, a therapist living in the Pacific Northwest and a stepmother for twenty-three years, put it this way:

> *When you are living in the midst of the sort of catastrophic mess that any stepfamily can become, you learn things about how far love can stretch if you just hang in there, or how purely awful, and then how strangely good, it can feel to love someone even when you are not fully loved in return. You learn, too, about your own nature, which is always more contradictory and paradoxical than ever seems possible. You learn about the lonely lunacy of hope. You learn that life isn't ever sterile or perfect and that that's okay; no, it's better than okay, it's wonderful.* (Family Therapy Networker, January/February 2000, p. 57)

Does living in a stepfamily *have* to be so hard? Not always, but most veterans of stepfamilies have stories to tell and memories of times when they wondered whether they, their partners, and their children would make it. Having the patience to "hang in there" and the skills to help you make good decisions and understand the process of stepfamily living can carry you through the chaos that sometimes happens—even among people who truly love each other.

Having these skills has become increasingly important. The truth is that combining families is a task more and more of us will face in the years ahead. As recently as fifty years ago, stepfamilies formed primarily because an adult lost a spouse to death and eventually remarried. In fact, the *step* in *stepfamily* and *stepparent* is commonly believed to come from an Old English term meaning "bereaved." Today, even though second and third marriages most commonly follow divorce, stepfamilies are still families born out of pain and loss.

Recent research shows us that somewhere between 50 and 60 percent of all first marriages will end in divorce. While some of these adults will remain single, 75 percent will eventually remarry. Experts who study family life estimate that 40 percent of the children in the United States will be part of at least one stepfamily at some point in their lives (Pasley et al., "Successful Stepfamily Therapy: Clients' Perspectives," *Journal of Marital and Family Therapy* 22, no. 3 [July 1996]). One out of every three Americans is now a stepparent, a stepchild, a stepsibling, or some other member of a stepfamily; more than half of Americans are now, have been, or eventually will be part of a stepfamily (Larson, "Understanding Stepfamilies," *American Demographics* 14, no. 360 [1992]). And because children often travel back and forth between separated parents, many children will be part of more than one stepfamily.

These rather staggering statistics generate all sorts of questions. If living in a blended family is complicated—and it inevitably is, at least for a while—how do adults and children survive, let alone thrive? Both children and adults may find themselves wondering, "Where do I fit in?" "Who's really in this family anyway?" "What if the kids only visit us instead of live with us?" "Who's in charge—of discipline, of money?" "Where should we live, and whose rules should be followed once we get there?" "How do we make sense of the differences in our old traditions and beliefs?" "How do we live together as a family when some of us barely know the rest of us?" "What do we do if we have ex-partners and other families to get along with?" These are complex questions, and they lead to one final, sobering statistic: At present, the failure rate for second and third marriages is even higher than for first marriages, as high as 65 to 70 percent in some estimates.

What does this all mean for you and for your children? Is it possible to build a stepfamily that works for all its members—a place where both adults and children can feel safe, loved, and free to grow and learn? Can stepparents and stepchildren live together in an atmosphere of mutual respect and dignity—and perhaps even genuine affection? The answer, we believe, is a hearty yes—with education, thoughtful planning, good communication skills, patience, and commitment.

This book will provide a basic blueprint for building a successful stepfamily; you must provide the desire and the courage. Rudolf Dreikurs spoke often about having the "courage to be imperfect." It may be wise to accept from the start that, while the wicked stepmother may be a myth, there are no "perfect" stepmothers (or stepfathers), either. It takes courage and determination to take on a job knowing that you will make mistakes. Yet mistakes are rarely fatal; they can be opportunities to learn and grow. We want to thank our friends, families, workshop participants, and many others we have encountered for sharing their stories and experiences so that others may learn from them. It may help you to know that others have faced the challenges of stepfamily living and have built homes where each member could feel belonging and warmth.

Adults and children living in stepfamilies will certainly face challenges together. The Chinese realized something long ago that may inspire us to keep going even when solving our problems seems beyond our strength. The ancient Chinese written character for *crisis* is a combination of the characters representing two other words: *danger* and *opportunity*. Each crisis that you face as parents, partners, children, and families contains both dangers and opportunities. You can learn from your mistakes and from each other. You can trust each other to grow and to create from the dangers you face opportunities to build a better life for yourself and those you love. Stepfamily homes can be wonderful places in which to live. Working and learning together, you can discover ways to make them so.

Dispelling the Myths and Fantasies About Stepfamilies

MANY DIFFERENT KINDS of families exist these days. The last half of the twentieth century brought unprecedented societal and lifestyle changes that profoundly altered the patterns of family life. Many people have bemoaned the "decline of the family" and mourned the disappearance of the old-fashioned Cleaver family, the Ozzie and Harriet version of family bliss that 1950s television convinced us was the norm. Our picture of family life in earlier decades was never entirely accurate, but there is no denying that the way Americans form families has changed.

Statistics tell us that there are now significantly more single-parent families, more families in which grandparents are raising their grandchildren, and more families headed by gay or lesbian couples than ever before. There are groups of friends and their children who have chosen to live together to support each other financially and emotionally. There are fewer traditional nuclear families—Mom, Dad, two kids, and the family dog. But stepfamilies are more common than any other type, and there are many misconceptions, myths, and mistaken ideas about stepfamilies that are so familiar we rarely stop to examine them.

Why? Well, one reason may be that stepfamilies are often seen as "second best." They also come in many forms and can be incredibly complex; each person involved may have his or her own perceptions about how the family ought to look. Take the Parker family, for example.

Joe and Ellen took their time deciding whether to marry. Joe's first wife had died of cancer after fourteen years of marriage and three children. Kyle, 12, Jennifer, 10, and Will, 6, missed their mom terribly. They wanted their dad to be happy and liked Ellen well enough when she came over for visits, but she just wasn't Mom. Sometimes they worried that accepting her might mean they had stopped loving their real mother. The more her memory faded, the more they fought to hang on to it. And that usually meant pushing Ellen away.

Ellen had never been married before. She liked Joe's children—or thought she did—but she was unsure whether she was ready to be an "instant mom." She hesitated marrying Joe but truly loved him and finally gave in, determined to win the children's love and create a happy, peaceful home.

In fact, Ellen may have tried a little too hard. The more affectionate she tried to be, the more the children withdrew. She tried to get them to talk, and they clammed up. She asked for their help, and they ignored her or talked back disrespectfully, rolling their eyes when they thought she couldn't see, although they seemed willing to do things for Joe. They did not like her cooking; they complained bitterly when she wanted to take down their mother's picture in the living room. Will seemed to enjoy Ellen's hugs and cuddles but retreated quickly when the older children glared at him.

Joe felt stuck in the middle. He loved Ellen and wanted his new family to be happy, but he understood his children's grief and their reluctance to accept a replacement for their mother. He, too, had precious memories of their time together and mourned her death. Holidays were tense. Joe's parents tried hard, but they had loved his first wife and missed her presence. The children wanted everything to be done "the way we used to." And Ellen's parents had a hard time accepting their "instant" grandchildren and wanted to know when Joe and Ellen planned to have a baby of their own. Everyone, it seemed, was unhappy.

Baby Jessica was born two years after Joe and Ellen's wedding. Ellen focused on her baby all of the love and attention Kyle, Jennifer, and Will hadn't wanted, and the older children immediately felt as excluded and rejected as Ellen had before. They enjoyed their new sister; it was sort of fun to hold and play with her. But it hurt, too, to see their dad and Ellen fussing together over the baby, and it made them miss their mother all over again.

Joe welcomed his new daughter, but his joy was tempered by his desire to avoid hurting Kyle, Jennifer, and Will. It was also hard to find time in his busy schedule for four children. Joe's parents were slow to warm up to the new addition and chose to spend their time with the three older children, while Ellen's parents showered the baby with kisses and presents. One night at dinner, while the baby cried and Jennifer complained that she hated peas and why did we have to have them *again,* Joe and Ellen gazed at each other across the table and wondered what had become of their dream of a happy new family. What could they possibly do to make this work?

> When a stepfamily begins, each member brings into it an entirely different set of feelings and fears.

Myths and Fantasies About Stepfamilies

MOST COUPLES BEGIN their first marriage with confidence and optimism. "Sure," they think, "we'll have hard times, but we love each other so much that we'll find a way to work things out." Even when reality sets in (and reality seldom lives up to the fantasies), problems are more likely to feel manageable. After all, only two people are involved. Children usually arrive one at a time, and the family has time to settle in and adjust to each new addition.

Couples who are marrying for a second time may also believe they are grounded in reality, but they usually harbor fantasies of their own, sometimes without realizing it. It is probably fantasy to believe that you won't take it personally if your stepchildren reject you. It is often fantasy to believe that you will love your stepchildren as much as you love your own (or even love them at all). It is usually fantasy to believe that every member of a stepfamily will be able to leave old beliefs and experiences behind and start fresh. It is fantasy to think your stepfamily will someday be perfect. Many stepparents do not even realize they have these fantasies until they experience the opposite: reality. In subsequent chapters we will examine the expectations and fears couples bring into their stepfamily and show how you might face and accept reality and use problems as opportunities for learning and growth.

No relationship (and no family) is without complications and challenges, but it's sometimes easier for beginners to chalk up their mistakes to inexperience, to forgive and try again. When a stepfamily begins, each member brings into it an entirely different set of feelings and fears. At least one adult has been through the loss of a partner, due to death, abandonment, or divorce. The children have memories of their first family and may feel confused about what to expect from the new one. Everyone involved soon learns that love isn't always enough, that troubles come and cannot always be solved.

When a nuclear family—the traditional one we described earlier—is viewed as "the way it ought to be," anything less (or even anything different) may seem to be failure. When you carry fears and expectations about what is possible, you may unconsciously create those things in your relationship. It is important to take a look at the ideas and beliefs you bring to your stepfamily.

A number of common myths about stepfamilies, stepparents, and stepchildren persist—ideas we have absorbed from our culture, from stories we have heard, and from our own assumptions. How much of what we believe is true? Let's look at a few common myths.

The Myth of the Wicked Stepmother and Cruel Stepfather

We have already taken a brief look at this one. While not all stepchildren feel toward their stepmothers the way Cinderella felt toward hers, the myth persists. It is not hard to understand why when you take a moment to investigate. Children may resent stepparents for a number of reasons, some of them quite good. Even the best-intentioned adult makes mistakes. A man may rush in too quickly to try to handle discipline issues with his stepchildren. If they haven't learned to accept and respect his position in the family, it is unlikely they will welcome his parenting. They may, in fact, decide to dislike him and resist him at every turn.

Adults sometimes resent the presence of children who are not theirs and with whom they share no history and feel no emotional bond. "I married Rick, not his kids," a woman may complain, "and I just wish they weren't around so often." Because children often use behavior to express their feelings and needs, adults who don't yet feel affection for those children can find their behavior difficult to accept—and may decide that they do not want a close relationship with such troublesome youngsters. When children sense their stepparent's emotional withdrawal, they may respond with more misbehavior and discouragement. Children are quick to sense rejection and dislike (or even uncertainty) and may return those feelings with extra intensity. Adults and children may find themselves caught in a dangerous, downward spiral, moving faster and faster away from love, trust, connection—and each other. It isn't difficult to understand why a new stepparent, even one who is "trying hard," can become the "wicked stepmother" or "cruel stepfather."

Adults need to realize that parents and children are a package deal; you can't marry one without the other. Still, a new spouse's children may not be easy to accept and love, or they may be very different from one's own children, making affection and enjoyment even more complicated. Partners may disagree about parenting, chores, and discipline; children who sense discord between the adults in their home may well decide that one of them is "the bad guy." The other adult may even agree!

The stepmother or stepfather is not always seen as the villain. Some children don't resent an "intruder" but, like the little boy in the movie *Sleepless in Seattle,* long for a new parent and become little matchmakers. They may even try to push their biological parent into marrying before he or she is ready. Sometimes it is the children who long for a new, happy family and who feel rejected when their efforts are not matched by those of their new stepparent. Just as not all stepparents are wicked, not all stepchildren are brats!

A basic fact of stepfamily living (and one that we will repeat often) is that trust, affection, and real relationships take time to build. Most adults admit that they expect family life to be harmonious and loving within a couple of months. Few are that fortunate! Being a stepparent is rarely easy, and learning to live peacefully with people you do not know well takes, at the very least, tremendous patience.

Are there real wicked stepmothers and cruel stepfathers? Perhaps. Are there perfect stepparents? Probably not. In fact, unfair as it may seem, trying too hard not to be a wicked stepparent might just make it happen. This leads us to the second of our myths about stepfamilies.

The Myth of Instant Love and Harmony

Stepfamilies usually begin when two adults fall in love. "Because we love each other," they may think, "we'll certainly love each other's children." The reality may prove somewhat different than the fantasy, however. Children who may have seemed absolutely adorable during an occasional dinner or afternoon picnic turn out to be utterly normal: They whine, bicker, cry, and sulk, seeming less and less adorable all the time. Many new stepparents do not have children of their own and find their assumptions about parenting are not accurate. Your new husband's 13-year-old daughter may pose quite a challenge when your only exposure to children has been a bit of baby-sitting when you were in high school!

Even experienced parents find the changes that occur when they combine families difficult to adjust to. A dad who is comfortable with his own boisterous, athletic son may find it difficult to understand his wife's quiet boy, who dreams of being a concert pianist. Stepsiblings may find they do not

> Adults need to realize that parents and children are a package deal; you can't marry one without the other.

particularly like each other or have anything in common, and they don't appreciate the competition for their own parent's attention. A woman may have longed for a little girl to love and may find the tomboy her new husband has raised impossible to deal with. A moment may come when new family members look at each other and realize, "I don't love this person; I'm not even sure I *like* this person!" Then they feel guilty and ashamed because, after all, aren't they supposed to love each other? Aren't they supposed to be a family now?

It would be wonderful if we could make love happen just because we want it to. You may love your partner very much and still find yourself unable to love his or her children as much as your own—or even at all. Does that mean your stepfamily is doomed? That depends on how these feelings are handled.

When life doesn't live up to our expectations, we sometimes believe something must be wrong with us or with the other people in our lives. It may be simply that we need more time, better skills, and a more realistic picture of what life in a stepfamily is all about. It could be that we need to learn that dignity, respect, and kindness are necessary and possible, no matter what our feelings. Love often follows respect. However, whether or not it leads to love, respect—along with simple courtesy—can make life not only tolerable but also enjoyable for everyone concerned. The suggestions in this book will be based on the importance of treating people with dignity and respect.

> You may love your partner very much and still find yourself unable to love his or her children as much as your own—or even at all.

Charles, for example, is an excellent stepfather. He spends time with his four-year-old stepson, Jon, takes turns with his new wife helping Jon get ready for preschool in the morning and fixing his breakfast, plays ball with him, and reads to him. Even though Charles acts just like a "real" father, he feels guilty that he does not have the same strong feelings of love for Jon that he has for his daughter, who lives in another state with his ex-wife.

Charles needs to know that it is normal to love your "birth children" more than your stepchildren. However, "more" need not be an issue when all children are treated respectfully. Charles will be happier when he is able to let go of his guilt, accept reality, and give himself credit for being the wonderful stepfather that he is.

The Myth That You Can Please Everyone

His kids love pizza and could eat it for every meal; her kids want steak or chicken. His kids love playing video games and watching movies on television; her kids prefer to read quietly or play outside. Last week his adolescent daughter got angry and decided to move to Mom's house; this week she's mad at Mom and wants to move back to Dad's. He wants to spend Thanksgiving with his parents while she wants to spend it with hers. Her kids want to visit their dad's parents. So the family eats three turkey dinners. Can you please everyone in a stepfamily? Should you even try?

Because you are on new and unfamiliar ground (and because most people fear rejection and failure), you may try to create closeness by satisfying everyone's desires. But not only is it unlikely that you can please everyone, even trying usually leads to chaos. Instead of creating happiness, you may wind up bickering and disagreeing. And no one wants more pain, do they? Isn't this new family supposed to be better? Shouldn't everyone be happy?

In even the healthiest and most loving families, parents and children do not agree all the time about everything. Many adults "know" that, yet they find the tension that exists in most new stepfamilies both uncomfortable and frightening. As we will see in the chapters ahead, small things—which television show the family watches, who sits next to whom—can take on hidden meanings in a stepfamily. And most adults, who truly want to please and make everyone feel comfortable, occasionally go overboard in trying to create feelings of goodwill. It may help you decide what is possible and reasonable if you understand from the beginning that there will be moments when some (or even all) of the members of your stepfamily aren't happy. With patience, effective parenting tools, and good communication skills, those uncomfortable moments will become fewer and fewer.

The Myth That the Stepfamily Will Make Up for Past Hurts

It is easy to believe that building a new family will somehow rescue us from the past. We all want to believe in starting over, in new beginnings, in making up for past mistakes. But what happens when we expect our new family to compensate us for our past losses?

Angela's divorce had been a painful one. Her ex-husband, Derek, had been violent and abusive; both she and her two children had spent much of their time with him feeling afraid. When she met Lyle, he seemed too good to be true. He was patient and understanding, talked easily with her about feelings and ideas, and though he had no children of his own, seemed willing to help her raise her two. "Finally," Angela thought, "I've found someone who can erase everything we suffered with Derek."

Despite all his wonderful qualities, however, Lyle turned out to be slightly less than perfect. He tried hard, but he was not used to children and had a tendency to yell. And when he did, the children immediately ran to find their mother. Angela found herself working overtime to keep Lyle from becoming angry at anything—and the more apologetic she was, the more impatient and dissatisfied he became. Angela had expected that Lyle would never be angry and found he could not live up to her expectations. "I thought you were different," she told him sadly. "I thought you could make us better."

> Finding wholeness is the task of each individual person; it is never something that another can give you, no matter how much you may love him or her.

The members of stepfamilies often have suffered loss and pain in past relationships, and it's only human to hope that this time around everything will be different. But it is not possible to wipe away memories of loss any more than to forget past joys and celebrations. It is, however, possible to learn from past mistakes and, most importantly, to heal. Finding wholeness is the task of each individual person; it is never something that another can give you, no matter how much you may love him or her. No person (and no relationship), no matter how good, can make up for the mistakes and injuries of the past. The pressure to be perfect can make stepfamily living unbearable for everyone.

The Myth That a Stepfamily Is Never As Good As a "Real" Family

This myth is, perhaps, the most persistent (and most subtle) of all. Most people dream of falling in love, marrying for life, raising children, and growing old together. When life doesn't turn out that way, they feel sad, disappointed, and sometimes bitter. What went wrong the first time? How can you accept and learn to live with the fact that your dreams did not come true? You may enter a second relationship and begin building a stepfamily determined not to make the same mistakes. It is frightening when you hit the inevitable bumps in the road. You cannot fail again—or can you? And even if this new family works, will it ever feel the same as your old one? Or, if the old one was disastrous, do problems in this new family mean a repeat performance? Can you ever recapture—or ever truly live—your dreams?

It isn't possible to re-create the past. Nor, most of the time, is that what people really want. What most stepfamilies are looking for is a feeling, the sense that they belong here, that they accept and respect each other, and that this new family truly is theirs. Perhaps it is wisest to look at stepfamilies clearly, to see them as what they really are: an entirely new and different thing for those involved. Some stepfamilies may always be tinged with a sense of loss, of unfulfilled dreams. But some are better than anything their members have experienced before—not perfect, perhaps, but much, much better. You can maintain your connections to your past—your memories, your experiences, and what you have learned from them—while continuing to focus on today, on making the family you have now the best it can be.

> Perhaps it is wisest to look at stepfamilies clearly, to see them as what they really are: an entirely new and different thing for those involved.

It may be a good idea to look for a moment at your own perceptions about stepfamilies. Myths only get in the way of creating something real, and they may keep you from recognizing the value of what you have. All families—of all types—have problems. They have both assets and liabilities. As we begin our journey toward creating an effective stepfamily, take a moment to be grateful for what you have and to identify the things you might like to improve.

Yes, stepfamilies can be complicated, and it takes time to feel comfortable. But it *is* possible. No one wants to be the wicked stepmother, the cruel stepfather, or a "brat"; no one wants to live with one. With a little effort, understanding, skills, and patience, no one has to!

What Exactly Is a Stepfamily?

IT SOUNDS DECEPTIVELY simple. A stepfamily, as we have defined it, means a family in which either or both adults bring one or more children from a previous relationship and decide to live together, perhaps adding children of their own as time goes on. In practice, however, stepfamilies are usually anything but simple. Stepfamilies come in a dizzying array of shapes and sizes, and even the people in them seldom stop to consider how complex they are. One way of understanding this is to draw a "map" of your new family.

Your Stepfamily Map

TO HELP YOU visualize your family, get a large piece of paper and some colored markers. Use circles to represent females and squares to represent males. In the middle of the paper draw a circle for Mom/Stepmom and write her name inside. Next to it draw a square for Dad/Stepdad and write his name inside. Connect these two with a line to represent their relationship. Draw other circles and squares on either side to represent previous spouses or relationships, with lines connecting them to circles and squares that represent children born to that couple. Add any children born in your stepfamily, children who may visit for the summer or weekends, grandparents, aunts and uncles, cousins, and other significant family members. It doesn't take long to realize how complicated this new family has become. Is it any wonder that both adults and children sometimes wonder where they belong?

In some stepfamilies, each adult brings his or her own children, while in others only the man or woman has children. In some families, all of the children are present all of the time, while in others some or all of the children are "visitors," arriving periodically to stay with one parent or the other. It is interesting to note that men with no children of their own report having the easiest time adjusting to stepfamily life, while women with no children of their own report having the hardest time. However, because each human being (and each family) is unique, there are no rules about what is easiest or best. What you have in your stepfamily is what you have, and any combination of adults and children can be wonderful—with some thoughtfulness, patience, and skill.

Your New Family: What Makes a Stepfamily Different?

Q: I just married a wonderful man after dating him for more than five years. I have two children. He has none of his own but has always gotten along very well with mine. Because we had been together for so long, I assumed that living together would be pretty easy, but ever since the wedding things have felt different. He and the kids argue about chores; he thinks they don't respect him. I feel caught between supporting him and protecting my kids, and I don't think I ever make everyone happy. Is living in a stepfamily always like this?

A: There may be folks out there who slip easily into stepfamily life without a single stumble, but they're few and far between. Many families discover that relationships that felt comfortable before marriage become more complicated when everyone tries to live together twenty-four hours a day, seven days a week. Stepfamilies are different; the loyalties and bonds that connect parents and children, husband and wife, are easily strained in the first months, even years, of life together. If you are aware of this up front, you won't feel shocked or disappointed. Instead, you can have a positive attitude about it. Look at every problem as an opportunity for learning and growing. Perhaps create a "detective game" and tell your children that you are looking for problems so you can learn and practice the skills for solving them. Focus on listening and acknowledging each person's feelings; involve everyone in finding solutions to problems as they arise. You cannot keep everyone happy, nor should you try. Time and patience will help everyone adjust to their new life together.

> Stepfamilies come in a dizzying array of shapes and sizes, and even the people in them seldom stop to consider how complex they are.

An important part of understanding your family is acknowledging that stepfamilies are different than original families. Successful stepfamilies have accepted—even embraced—that fact. Living in a stepfamily becomes far more difficult when you blindly accept the myths and misconceptions or fail to recognize that stepfamilies experience a developmental process that may feel uncomfortable but is actually quite normal. The Accepting the Differences box outlines some of the ways that stepfamilies are different (not worse, just different!) than first families.

If you expect your stepfamily to look, feel, and function just like an original, biological family, you will undoubtedly be disappointed. But differences need not lead to disagreements. Accepting your stepfamily for what it is will also help you see its potential to become something wonderful. You can learn to work on the challenges your family faces while maintaining your hope and commitment to your partner and the children you share.

ACCEPTING THE DIFFERENCES: STEPFAMILIES AND ORIGINAL FAMILIES

Original Family	Stepfamily
• Both partners are starting fresh, with high hopes and expectations.	• Each partner has a history, which may include death of or divorce from previous partner.
• The couple learns to run a household, manage finances, and solve problems.	• Each partner has his or her own ideas and experiences about how things "should be done" together.
• The couple creates its own set of traditions and builds a history together.	• Each partner arrives with separate traditions and rituals.
• Children arrive one at a time, usually with several years in between.	• Children are present at the beginning of the family; there is little or no time to adjust.
• Parents build a parenting philosophy together and share a lifelong history with their children.	• Parents and stepparents may disagree about parenting; neither has been part of the other's history with his or her children and may feel excluded.
• Loyalties are generally straight-forward and evolve over time.	• Loyalties are complicated and may involve people outside the home.
• Both parents have legal and moral rights regarding the children.	• Legal rights and roles are often unclear.
• Children live in one home with their parents.	• Children may travel between households that have different rules and expectations.

Making It Work: The Traits of Healthy Families

AS WITH MOST things in life, stepfamilies have both assets and liabilities. Still, the complexity can be confusing. (How, for instance, do you work out who is responsible for chores when some children are only around some of the time?) Even when stepfamilies are complicated, though, they provide members with an opportunity to learn different ways of looking at life and of doing things; they expand the family's resources by adding new and interesting people. What are the assets—present and potential—of your family? What are the liabilities?

> If you expect your stepfamily to look, feel, and function just like an original, biological family, you will undoubtedly be disappointed.

One asset we all possess in blending a family is the opportunity to create a family that works for the people in it. It need not look like anyone else's family, and it need not be like any you've known before. We have all heard the term *dysfunctional family,* and no one wants to experience one! But what makes a family healthy? How do you build your family so it becomes the best it can possibly be?

Interestingly enough, a great deal of research has been done on precisely this subject. Those who have studied strong, healthy families (Stinnett and Sauer 1977; Sanders 1979; Stinnett and DeFrain 1985) have identified a number of qualities that they have in common. While the lists vary a bit, almost all include the same six important qualities: commitment, mutual appreciation, communication, time, spirituality, and coping ability. These appear to be the traits that make a family strong. What do they look like in a stepfamily?

Commitment

Commitment seems an obvious ingredient. But in a world where half of all marriages end in divorce and where some children never know both parents, we have learned that "'til death do us part" simply doesn't always happen.

Commitment is important. Men and women in the process of pledging their love and loyalty to a new partner want to believe that their partners and family members are as interested as they are in making this new family work—

and as willing to invest their energy and time. They usually want to be reassured that those they love and depend on won't disappear at the first sign of trouble. In a stepfamily, one or both of the adults involved has experienced the end of a previous relationship, which can make wholehearted commitment to a new family especially tricky.

"I married Jan because she's a great lady and I love her," Kevin said, "but I know there will be problems, especially when her kids come to visit. I've already survived the end of one relationship; I guess I can survive again if this one doesn't work." While Kevin's attitude may be understandable, Jan will almost certainly know that his commitment to their marriage is tentative. How will that affect her commitment to him?

Expectations have a lot to do with commitment. If your expectations include the fantasy of a perfect person or a perfect relationship, your commitment may wane when reality sets in. If you expect others to change in order to live up to your expectations, you may feel justified in giving up on your commitment when that doesn't happen. On the other hand, if you have sufficient tolerance, compassion, and respect for differences—and the skills to deal respectfully with differences—commitment grows. It is especially helpful if you can learn to see problems as opportunities for growth and if you develop the skills to find solutions to the problems.

> Stepfamilies provide opportunities to learn different ways of looking at life and of doing things.

Relationships do not come with guarantees, and none of us gets to know in advance what the future holds. Most of us have some healing to do from past hurts. But our families will have the best chance of succeeding when we summon the faith and courage to devote ourselves to them, to make a heartfelt commitment to the people we love and to the family we are creating, to see things through, and to work things out, "for better or for worse."

Mutual Appreciation

Most folks, when given the chance, are pretty good at pointing out what's wrong, what needs to be different, or what others around them need to improve. How often, though, do you take the time to notice what's right? How often do you tell those you love and live with what you appreciate about them?

We will have more to say about mutual appreciation later in this book, but it's worth saying several times: People generally do better when they feel better, and they often feel better when they believe they are appreciated for who they are, as well as for the things they do. The healthiest families are those in which people express gratitude to each other, encourage each other, and celebrate positive things about each other.

> If you have sufficient tolerance, compassion, and respect for differences, then commitment grows.

For example, as part of their commitment to their new stepfamily, the Fallons decided to teach their children to be "good finders." At their first family meeting, they gave each member a small notebook and a challenge: "See how many good things you can find about our family and about everyone in it, and write them down in your notebook. At our next family meeting, we'll read aloud what we have found and save our comments in our 'appreciations box.'" They then presented the children with a large cardboard box, old magazines, scissors, and glue. The children soon forgot their fears and shyness as they searched for pictures in magazines to decorate their new family's appreciations box.

Charlie Shedd pointed out in *Letters to Karen*, "A person's faults are the price you pay for their virtues." Too often couples focus on the positive aspects of a trait when they "fall in love," and then focus on the negative aspects of a trait after the honeymoon is over. What was once seen as solid and dependable might later be seen as boring; what was once seen as exciting enthusiasm might later be seen as flighty behavior. It helps to remember and focus on the positive aspects of personality traits. Think for a moment about how the atmosphere in your stepfamily might improve if everyone in it acquired the habit of noticing the positives and actually saying something about them. It is exciting to realize that mutual appreciation is a skill that can be learned—and taught. We will explore that further in chapter 10.

Communication

Emma was late—again. A confrontation with her 15-year-old daughter, Carmen, was definitely not what she needed this morning, but it looked as though she wasn't going to get a choice in the matter.

"Mom," Carmen said, poking her head into her mother's bathroom, "can we go to the mall tonight? I really need some new shoes, and I want to spend my birthday money on some new CDs."

Emma sighed. "We can't, Carmen—not tonight. Your brother has a soccer game, and we promised to go. Anyway, you should spend your money on some new clothes. Those jeans have holes in them."

Carmen's eyes flashed dangerously. "Ryan isn't my brother—he's just my stepbrother. I don't want to go to his stupid soccer game. You're supposed to be my mom—you're supposed to do things with me. But ever since you married Bob, all you care about is his kid and his stuff—you never have time for me anymore. You promised twice last week to take me to the mall, and both times you didn't keep your promise. Besides, I like the holes in my jeans."

> Healthy families are those in which people express gratitude to each other, encourage each other, and celebrate positive things about each other.

Emma put down her mascara and faced her angry daughter. "I'm sorry about last week, but you should try to be more understanding of Ryan. He's had a hard time since his parents' divorce. I expect you to be more mature—

you're older. But you haven't been much help to me lately, Carmen. I'm trying to make this marriage work, and you're causing nothing but problems."

"Fine!" Carmen shouted, tears springing into her eyes. "I just won't bother you any more!" Emma heard the door slam behind her daughter and sighed. Why did things always have to be so complicated?

Emma and Carmen were both doing lots of talking, but how much real communication was taking place? It's doubtful that either felt understood. Let's replay this scene and see what it would look like if Mom practiced effective communication skills.

"Mom," Carmen said, poking her head into her mother's bathroom, "can we go to the mall tonight? I really need some new shoes, and I want to spend my birthday money on some new CDs."

Emma sighed. "We can't, Carmen—not tonight. Your brother has a soccer game and we promised to go. Let's look at the calendar and schedule a time when we can go to the mall together."

Carmen's eyes flashed dangerously. "Ryan isn't my brother—he's just my stepbrother. I don't want to go to his stupid soccer game. You're supposed to be my mom—you're supposed to do things with me. But ever since you married Bob, all you care about is his kid and his stuff—you never have time for me anymore. You promised twice last week to take me to the mall, and both times you didn't keep your promise."

Emma focused on the hurt Carmen was expressing. "I'm sorry about last week. I guess I didn't realize how much I have been neglecting you. Thank you for telling me. Now let's be sure to put a time on the calendar, and I will mark it top priority."

"But I want to go *now!*" Carmen said, tears springing into her eyes. "It seems to me that everyone else is more important to you than I am!"

Emma took a deep breath to get some self-control, avoided defensiveness, validated Carmen's feelings, and focused on solutions. "I can see how it might seem that way to you. I have certainly made some mistakes. I think we can both do better. Deal?"

Somewhat mollified, Carmen shook her mom's hand. "Okay. Deal."

Again, Emma focused on a solution, instead of getting hooked into defensive explanations. "Okay. Now let's get out the calendar and a purple pen for top priority."

COMMUNICATION THAT CREATES CLOSENESS AND TRUST, NOT DISTANCE AND HOSTILITY

We examine communication skills in greater detail in chapter 8. For now, here is a brief summary of the skills Emma used to reach closeness with Carmen instead of distance and hostility:

1. Emma paid more attention to the feelings being expressed than to the words.

2. She validated Carmen's feelings instead of becoming defensive.

3. She took responsibility and apologized for her part in Carmen's hurt feelings.

4. She focused on listening instead of on explaining.

5. She avoided "side tent" issues and focused on the "main tent" issue: Carmen's hurt feelings (not her attacks on her mother, stepfather, and stepbrother).

6. She avoided lectures and judgments about Carmen's clothes and how she should spend her birthday money (more "side tent" issues).

7. She kept working for resolution of the conflict by finding solutions to the real problems.

Communication skills are vitally important tools in helping people get along, understand one another's needs, and solve problems, but they are often skills we haven't had the opportunity to learn and practice. Most families, "step" or otherwise, recognize that they need to learn to listen and to speak in ways others can hear. Healthy families communicate; they share ideas and concerns, solve problems effectively, and listen well and often.

Time

Ask most people these days what they wish they had more of, and they'll usually give you one of two answers: time or money. Money undoubtedly makes life easier, but it is time that helps families become strong.

> Time should be budgeted, much as we budget our money, and should be invested in the things we believe are important.

Healthy families spend time together. They have learned to appreciate the value of living "in the moment" and have made one another a priority in budgeting time. Especially in stepfamilies, in which members may not yet know each other well, spending time together is a wise investment in building strong relationships. Not coincidentally, managing time well alleviates a great deal of stress, which is among the most common causes of family problems. It is important, too, to examine your priorities and to determine the difference between needs and wants. Many couples have found that while they were spending their time working for the bigger house and better vacation, the interests and emotions that connected them in the first place withered away.

A calendar is an important part of every family meeting (which we will learn more about in chapter 9). Take time to list all special events while everyone is there to participate. Get everyone involved in the juggling act. Who can drive where and when? Who can take turns attending important functions when not everyone can be there? What needs to be written in a special color for top priority?

Time can—and should—be budgeted, much as we budget our money, and should be invested in the things we believe are important. Your new family is worth the investment of your time and energy, isn't it?

Spirituality

Many people treat spirituality and religion as synonymous. A famous theologian once defined spirituality as "an active sense of identification with something greater than oneself that gives life meaning and purpose." Under this definition, many things religious may not be spiritual, and many things spiritual may not be religious; but such things as service to others, patriotism, a belief in God or a higher power, and concern for the Earth and the environment may be essentially spiritual in nature. (In reality, many religious people are not spiritual, and many spiritual people are not religious.)

> What matters is not what sort of spiritual life a family has but simply that it does indeed have one.

For most people, a spiritual life is a source of strength, a foundation on which to build, and a way of finding connection and community. It is interesting to note that research tells us that what matters is not what sort of spiritual life a family has but simply that it does indeed have one. Families tend to be stronger and to do better when they share faith in something greater than themselves.

For stepfamilies, though, this may be easier said than done. The members of your stepfamily may have come from different religious traditions and faiths. New partners may have to decide how they will raise their children, what traditions they will follow, or how to blend their different beliefs into a functioning whole while still respecting each individual.

We certainly do not intend to give spiritual advice; each individual (and each family) must explore this territory for him- or herself. But giving some thought to your family's spiritual life may provide added strength to the foundation on which you are building.

The family meeting could offer an excellent time to explore what spirituality will mean to your family. Let all members take turns sharing what they would like. One family decided to begin every family meeting with something spiritual. Each member took turns presenting a spiritual quote, a reading, music, art, or an inspirational story.

Another stepfamily decided that each member would take turns choosing a local church to visit on Sundays. They then evaluated their experience at the next family meeting. They kept doing this until they found a church that everyone liked, and that place became "their" church.

One family found itself quite deeply divided by different religious commitments but learned that they were united in a concern for the Earth. They

decided to respect each other's different beliefs with respect to God and even attended special events with each other's religious groups. They then made a family commitment to the Earth and the environment. They began by recycling, went on to studying environmental issues, then to supporting groups and activities that reflected their new family cause.

All these families were creating their own traditions and uniqueness. They worked together to determine the new instead of fighting over the old.

Coping Ability

If you haven't already learned this one, here is the news: Change is inevitable. Every stepfamily in existence has learned the importance of flexibility, tolerance, and the ability to find new ways of doing things. Families who succeed are able to cope, to adjust to change. A wise person once said that, to the beginner, there are many possibilities in life; to an expert, there are only a few. If you can remember that mistakes are opportunities to learn and remember to be a "beginner," you will usually find ways of getting along. You may even discover that the changes you most feared and struggled with have brought you the greatest growth—and a better life.

> Families who succeed are able to cope, to adjust to change.

One of the quickest paths to conflict is to insist on being "right." In addition, many stepfamilies have discovered that the little things tend to be the issues that lead to disagreement. Whose kids will take out the trash? Which utensils go in which kitchen drawers? How will you arrange the furniture—and whose furniture will you arrange? Many stepfamilies find themselves approaching differences as though there must be a winner and a loser, but this approach rarely leads to harmony and contentment—even if you "win" most of the time. By learning to focus on solutions rather than blame, you can help your family develop the flexibility and respect to cope with change and difference and to find win/win answers that work for everyone. We will explore ways to focus on solutions as we continue through this book.

Does any family ever "get it all together"? Does any family possess all these qualities? Well, we all possess each of them to some degree. All these traits of successful families exist on a continuum; most families are doing well at some and need to work on others. Simply put, all families (and, perhaps, especially stepfamilies) require mutual respect and dignity to be healthy. We all want to belong, to feel valued and significant. We want the people we love to feel that way, too. How can we make that happen?

What Do You Want Your Stepfamily to Look Like?

SIT QUIETLY FOR just a moment and think: What sort of family would you really like to have? Ask your partner; ask your children. What are the things all of you value, that you would like to experience in your home? Take the time to write down what you discover; post your family goals on the refrigerator and invite family members to add to it.

> All too often, we spend less time planning our family life than planning a long trip.

If you were going to start out on a long journey to a place you had never visited, chances are good that you would do some planning. You would probably decide on a route and on a means of getting there. If you decided to drive, you would be wise to check the car and to sit down with a map. You might determine what tools to take with you and spend some time preparing for bad weather and problems you anticipate along the way.

All too often, however, we spend less time planning our family life than planning a long trip. Stepfamilies in particular may embark on their journey together in a haze of hope and expectation without fully examining the details of their life together. If the list of goals you have written down is your destination, how will you get there? How can you help your family become the kind of family all of you want it to be? What tools will you need to deal with problems along the way?

Stepfamilies have many parts; they contain a couple, various combinations of children, and extended family members. We'll begin by exploring the new couple's world and move on through the issues the family is likely to face, together and as individuals. As we go along, keep your own family firmly in mind. You will discover the tools, skills, and understanding to make your journey together a successful one.

3

The New Couple

The Foundation of the Stepfamily

NEAL SAT STARING out his office window at the busy street below, thinking once again about Sharon. He smiled when he remembered those first heady weeks, knowing he was in love again—at last!—and thoroughly enjoying the feeling. The smile faded a bit as he thought about the past few months.

Sharon was special. She was bright, energetic, and affectionate; she was athletic and fun-loving; and Neal enjoyed having a partner he could ski, run, and work out with. Both Sharon and Neal had been married before; each had a nine-year-old son. In fact, they had met when their boys' Little League teams had played each other. And, miracle of miracles, the two boys got along well and genuinely enjoyed the time they had to hang out together.

He had waited a whole two years to ask her to marry him, even though he'd known from the beginning that she was the best thing to happen to him in years. Sharon had calmed him down; he felt secure and optimistic when she was around. Still, he wanted to be sure. After all, his divorce had been messy and painful, and he had no desire to go through that ever again.

Their wedding, with the two boys as grinning attendants, had been lots of fun; the honeymoon had been perfect. Because Sharon's home was larger than Neal's was (and because money was tight and buying a new home seemed out of the question), he and his son had moved in with her and her boy. Almost immediately, life had become tense and complicated.

Oh, they had expected some problems with the boys as they worked out new rules and agreed on their territory, but there had been surprisingly little to worry about on that front. No, it was he and Sharon who were struggling.

Neal sighed. He felt like an intruder. He hadn't realized until he moved into Sharon's home how different their lifestyles were. He enjoyed relaxing in front of the television at the end of the day, while Sharon preferred music and a magazine. He hadn't thought furniture and knickknacks would be important to him, but he found he missed his familiar, comfortable things, and Sharon's carefully arranged decor did not seem to have room for his lumpy armchair and battered desk. The way he shopped for groceries, cooked a meal, and arranged his things in their closet annoyed his wife, and he found her fussiness equally frustrating.

> A stable, healthy couple is far better equipped to build a stable, healthy stepfamily.

Before their marriage, they had been able to talk about problems; but now it seemed that every time he mentioned his concerns to Sharon, she either withdrew or got defensive and irritable. Each felt criticized by the other, and Neal felt himself digging in his heels; he didn't want to compromise anymore, and, apparently, neither did Sharon. Last night he and Sharon had hardly talked; now Neal was worried. This had happened with his first wife, too. Was *this* marriage doomed to fail? Was there something wrong with him? With her? How could such small problems feel so large? Maybe he just wasn't any good at relationships.

Neal sighed again and pushed himself away from his desk. He would go to the gym on his way home. He could watch the game on the overhead television while he exercised, and maybe Sharon would be in a better mood by the time he got home. Maybe. . . .

The Importance of the Couple's Relationship

ALL COUPLES HAVE problems from time to time; most of us accept that. But for remarrying couples, even small problems can seem dangerous and disturbing. Conventional wisdom tells us that a couple's relationship sets the tone for their family; this point seems especially true of stepfamilies. In fact, most stepfamily members know instinctively that a stepparent's commitment to his or her stepchildren is conditional, based on the success of the marriage itself; "step" relationships rarely continue if the couple's relationship does not.

Adults remarry for a variety of reasons. Sometimes they are looking primarily for financial security or a new parent for their children; sometimes they want a truly satisfying relationship with another adult. Sometimes they want "all of the above"! A stable, healthy couple is far better equipped to build a stable, healthy stepfamily. But how do you know whether your relationship is healthy? How do you know whether you're even ready to begin again? And what should you do if you discover that you have more problems than you thought? Does a second (or third) marriage have to be hard work?

Relationships are among life's greatest challenges. Nowhere else in our life's journey do we learn more about ourselves, have more potential to grow and learn, or risk more. Relationships—with partners, parents, children, friends, and colleagues—form the fabric of our lives. Yet few of us have anything but on-the-job training to teach us how to create truly healthy relationships. Most of what we know comes from watching those around us and from trial and error—lots of error! Mistakes are wonderful opportunities to learn, but wouldn't it be nice if there were an easier way?

Opening the "Box"

BETTY'S BELOVED HUSBAND died suddenly of a heart attack; she and her new husband both have fears that he might not be able to measure up. Stan's marriage ended in a bitter divorce; he tries to hide his fear that his new marriage might end the same way. Jack's ex-wife was an abusive parent; he wonders whether he should allow his new wife to be alone with his children or to discipline them. Mary's first husband left her for another woman; she tries to hide fears that she is not good enough and that men can't be trusted.

A second (or third) marriage may be built on the shaky foundation of leftover fears and expectations from previous relationships. New partners may find themselves unwittingly dealing with memories and stereotypes from the past instead of the real people in the present or repeating familiar but ineffective patterns. How can you avoid this trap? Perhaps each of us should wear a sign declaring, "I'm *me,* not your ex!"

Imagine, for a moment, a box. Perhaps it looks like a small treasure chest; perhaps it is enameled and studded with precious gems or made of ragged cardboard. Each person carries such a "box" deep inside, a special place where you keep your memories, your souvenirs of the past, and the decisions about yourself and others that you have made throughout your life. Often the box is heavy; its contents drag you down, color your thoughts and perceptions, and keep you from having the relationships and family life you dream of. Understanding the patterns you create in your relationships, the mistakes you make, and the ways you unthinkingly react to stress or a challenge can help you approach new relationships in new, more effective ways. At some point, continuing to grow as a person, as a parent, and as part of a couple means opening your box and examining what you find there.

> Respect may be the single most important quality of healthy relationships.

By the time we reach adulthood, each of us has accumulated a wealth of subconscious thoughts, feelings, and conclusions about ourselves, others, and what we need to do to find belonging and significance. These conclusions contribute to our perceptions and influence our behavior and the patterns we follow in our relationships. What does your box look like? What is in it? And how do you get rid of the bits and pieces that no longer work for you?

Personality Differences

You may have noticed that some of what you find in your box is unpleasant, while other items bring back happy memories and give you a great deal of joy. Buried in your box are the fears and expectations you bring to your current relationship and your individual personality style. Even when a couple has addressed and dealt with their fears and expectations, they still are faced with their basic personality differences. Couples seem to do very well when each person can respect both her own needs and feelings and those of her partner; couples get into trouble when they adopt a right/wrong mentality about them. And when couples are not being respectful, they are both "wrong"!

John Gottman, Ph.D., a professor of psychology at the University of Washington and the founder and director of the Seattle Marital and Family Institute, has spent years studying couples and their interactions. He has identified four behaviors that pose a serious risk to marriage and relationships: criticism, contempt, defensiveness, and stonewalling (refusing to talk about or deal with an issue) (Gottman and Silver 1999). You may agree that these are serious problems for couples; you may even acknowledge that you do one or more of them. But why? Why do you (and the rest of us) so often behave in ways that make your life with those you love more difficult?

Throughout our lives, from earliest childhood to the present moment, you have made decisions about yourself and others. These decisions—about how you must find safety, belonging, and significance, about families and marriage, about who you are and what your possibilities might be—influence every aspect of your life as a partner and as a parent. But some sources and events, such as those we will discuss next, have had a particularly strong effect on your personality and the person you have become.

Your Original Family

When you were a child, your family was your entire world. You watched your parents and siblings constantly for clues about life and how to live it. You didn't learn until much later that the family down the street did things differently. Your original family taught you their version of what men and women are or should be. They taught you about relationships and trust, and, perhaps most important, they taught you who you are and where you fit in. Your perception of an event (rather than the historical "truth") and what you decided about that perception are more significant than what actually happened.

You have made many decisions, usually subconsciously, about yourself: Are you good, bad, capable, incapable, loved, unloved? You make decisions about the world: Is it safe or dangerous, scary or full of wonder? You make decisions about others: Are they supportive or critical, forgiving or judgmental, nurturing or threatening? Based on these decisions you created some "only if" decisions. For example:

> "I'm incapable, so I will survive *only if* I don't take risks where my
> failures will be obvious."
> "I'm incapable, so I will survive *only if* I become more capable than
> anyone else."
> "I belong *only if* others treat me as though I'm special and take care
> of me."
> "I belong *only if* I'm in charge."

These are just a few of the millions of decisions that could be made by different individuals.

A couple may find that they are attracted to one another in the beginning because she likes to be taken care of and he likes to be in charge. However, the problems begin when she feels too controlled, and/or he gets tired of her helplessness. Too many couples in relationships blame one another instead of taking a look at the decisions each of them has made that may have made sense when they were young, but are no longer useful. By the time a child is five years old, he has usually decided whether he is smart, loved, cute, or an annoyance that people wish would go away. One of the ironies of life is that children grow up to be adults who act in ways that support what they already believe about themselves—even when it is not true. When they marry, those now-

grown children begin building a life with another person who may have an entirely different set of beliefs, decisions, and perceptions. It's no wonder relationships can be so confusing!

Most adults spend a lifetime examining and sorting through—knowingly or unknowingly—what they've learned from their original family. What have you decided? Which things in your own box do you want to keep? What might you want to do differently? You may find it helpful to spend some time pondering these questions about your childhood; in fact, recording your thoughts and feelings in a journal (and, perhaps, sharing them with your partner) may prove to be extremely valuable in understanding your relationships, past and present. Take a moment to open the box:

> What are some messages you heard about yourself from your parents
>   and siblings?
> What are some messages you heard about women? About men?
> What are the messages (by word or action) you heard about marriage?
> What did you decide about yourself and marriage?
> How have the decisions you made as a child affected your current
>   relationship?

For example, Shelly's mother told her again and again, "You could do so much better if you would just try." Shelly's older sisters were critical and often made fun of her; her parents kept an uneasy peace, mainly by avoiding each other. Shelly made several subconscious decisions. She decided that her sisters were right: She couldn't do anything very well. She stopped trying very hard so she would never be disappointed by failure, and she kept her distance from her own husband, avoiding conflict but also missing the opportunity for real connection.

Shelly doesn't realize that she keeps creating what she fears in her new stepfamily. When she worries that she "isn't good enough," she behaves as though she is not—and then feels upset when her husband and stepchildren treat her according to

> One of the ironies of life is that children grow up to be adults who act in ways that support what they already believe about themselves—even when it is not true.

her belief. Instead of loving others, she worries about being loved—and then wonders why others get impatient with her neediness. Her subconscious decision to protect herself from disappointment by not trying too hard has a big impact on her family. Instead of doing what she can to improve her marriage and understand her stepchildren, she passively watches the family fall apart, thus proving that she was right about herself all along.

Your First Relationship

Adults who are creating a stepfamily usually have been married before or have had at least one serious relationship. You have learned things from this experience, too. In a first marriage, some couples evolve together. They learn about trust and communication; they experience sexuality and discover what it means to them. They may build a home, pursue a career, and have children. Others, unfortunately, learn more about distrust than trust, lack of communication than honest expression of thoughts and feelings. They expect their partner to "make them happy," and they find either satisfaction or disappointment. Either way, they make more decisions about themselves and others.

Many people unwittingly choose a partner whom they believe possesses qualities they lack; ironically, those very qualities may become the things they find most annoying later and want to change. When a relationship ends and the dream is shattered, you learn and decide things about who you are now and what you believe you must do to find love and belonging again. You gather up what you have learned and place it in the box.

The Ending and Aftermath of a Relationship

Ending a relationship is rarely easy. Has anyone ever told you how much she enjoyed her divorce? Even when separation is best for both adults, dismantling a home can be terribly painful, especially when children are involved. It is a rare person who can endure the process of settling property and visitation issues, and dividing up the memories, without placing some heavy items in the box.

Of course, not all relationships end in divorce. Losing a partner to death creates different emotions and different decisions. Learning to trust and love again may be just as difficult for widowed as for divorced adults; it also may be tough for a new spouse to live up to the memory of Saint Jake or Saint Sandra.

As they face new relationships, most adults discover they need to deal with their accumulated decisions about trust, intimacy, and vulnerability. Learning to be a single parent or adjusting to financial changes brings new learning as well. When two adults merge their individual lives and histories, accumulated decisions and emotions can feel overwhelming, especially because they are rarely acknowledged or discussed openly.

Facing the Past

EACH ADULT CARRIES a box inside him- or herself; each of us has a life-time of accumulated experiences and perceptions. As we have seen, though, partners who join their separate families into one often find fears and expecta-tions among the contents of their boxes. There is nothing wrong with having fears or expectations, but you may get yourself into trouble when you are un-aware of them or choose not to talk about them.

Remember Neal and Sharon? Both had formed many subconscious beliefs about themselves and what they needed from their relationship. Both had fears about remarriage, and both had expectations for themselves and their partner. Because their courtship had gone so smoothly, it had been easy to shove these troubling thoughts aside. As Neal drove home from the gym later that evening, he realized that the problems he and Sharon were experiencing weren't fatal, but that they would require thought and work. He loved Sharon very much—he was certain of that—and he resolved to find a way to make their relation-ship stronger. Part of the work was his alone; Neal was beginning to wonder whether he'd recovered from his first marriage as completely as he had thought.

Achieving an Emotional Divorce

WE RECOGNIZE THAT many adults who contemplate forming a stepfamily have not been through a divorce. Losing a partner to death leaves its own scars and memories, as does abandonment or the absence of any committed

relationship. We do not intend to minimize the feelings of those who have endured such pain or the difficulties of their situation.

Still, we must focus on divorce for a moment because the vast majority of adults who remarry have survived a divorce, and divorce inevitably creates a multitude of emotional and legal complications (for both adults and children). Physically separating from a partner may be painful, but eventually a day does dawn when you are on your own. Your belongings are packed; all of the papers have been signed. Unfortunately, the emotional bonds connecting you to a former spouse or partner are often much harder to dissolve than the legal ones.

Although each individual's experience is unique, grieving the loss of a relationship, overcoming anger and hurt, and learning to live life on one's own generally take anywhere from two to five years. During that time, many things may remind you of a former love, and many things can happen to reopen the old wounds. Many men and women remarry within a few years of a divorce. Many have not truly completed the healing process and find it difficult to approach a new relationship in healthy ways.

Simply put, the process of healing takes as much time as it takes; it is important to be patient and gentle with yourself. The following box contains questions that may help you decide whether you can enter a new relationship with your whole heart or whether you still have some healing to do.

The emotional attachment (both negative and positive) to a former mate can seriously impede the development of a healthy relationship in the present. You may not believe you have any tie to your former partner, but think for a

ARE YOU STILL BOUND TO YOUR FORMER MATE?

- Are you uncomfortable seeing your former partner?

- Do you have difficulty talking to him or her calmly?

- Are you still trying to please your former mate?

- Does your former partner still make you angry?

- Do you want revenge or to make friends and family choose sides?

- Do you think of your former partner often?

- Does your former partner still enter your home as though he or she belongs there?

- Do you look for similarities and differences between your former and your current mate?

- Do you have difficulty talking calmly with your current partner about your former partner?

- Do you have difficulty accepting your former mate's new relationships?

A yes answer to any of these questions may indicate that you have not yet achieved an "emotional divorce."

moment: Anger, resentment, and bitterness are often as strong a bond as love. The healing process is different for each of us, but exploring your own feelings and experiences will help you discover for yourself whether you are ready to move forward or still need to make peace with the past—and let go of it.

When Neal arrived home, Sharon was waiting at the door with a sheepish smile and a hug. "I'm sorry," she said. "I know I've been hard to live with lately. It's just that I feel so confused sometimes about how things should be. I don't want to give up too much of my space. And," Sharon hesitated a moment, "sometimes I'm afraid. It seems easier to just shut you out than deal with all these fears and feelings."

Neal hugged her again. "I know," he said. "Me, too. But I really want this marriage to last, honey. Can we work together on ways to feel more comfortable and to get along better?"

Neal and Sharon decided to find a counselor who could help them learn to have the sort of relationship (and family) they wanted for themselves and their sons. They recognized that they could solve their problems and learn to respect their differences and that the process might be easier with help.

> There is nothing wrong with having fears or expectations, but you may get into trouble when you are unaware of them or choose not to talk about them.

Understanding and healing old beliefs can be very beneficial for a couple. Instead of letting things crowd the box you carry within you, it might be time to do some unpacking—not only of inaccurate childhood beliefs but also of fears and memories from previous relationships. Many of the following suggestions are simple (and are sometimes dismissed for exactly that reason), but never underestimate the power of simple ideas.

Building Blocks for a Loving, Respectful Relationship

YOU AND YOUR partner might consider these suggestions to help you create a loving, respectful relationship.

1. Take a moment to look inside. What fears do you bring to this new relationship? What expectations do you have of yourself? Of your partner? Can you talk calmly together about these things? If you can, you may discover that your fears lose much of their power. You may also be able to discard unrealistic expectations (remember those fantasies we talked about?) and work with your partner to meet the realistic ones.

2. Be open to trust and intimacy. Fear creates walls. Sadly, some couples find they are so focused on protecting themselves (or so focused on winning their partner's approval) that they are never able to break the walls down completely. Real trust—the willingness to be vulnerable and genuine—takes time, especially if you have been hurt before.

In his excellent book *Passionate Marriage: Keeping Love and Intimacy Alive in Committed Relationships* (Owl Books, 1998), David Schnarch, Ph.D., explores the idea that true intimacy happens when each partner can take care of him- or herself *and* remain close and connected to a partner. Marriage, he says, is a "people-growing machine" and by its very nature forces couples to confront themselves. The process can be uncomfortable; most couples believe that anxiety is a signal that something is wrong in their relationship, but real growth usually means learning to tolerate discomfort—and even pain—in the process of learning trust and intimacy. The result—a loving and respectful relationship—is worth the investment.

> Grieving the loss of a relationship, overcoming anger and hurt, and learning to live life on one's own can take anywhere from two to five years.

3. Practice mutual respect. Respect may be the single most important quality of healthy relationships. Mutual respect means valuing both yourself and your partner, treating both yourself and your partner well. It means taking responsibility for your own feelings, as well as being willing to listen to your partner's. It means working toward cooperation instead of competition and learning to value each person's uniqueness rather than insisting on sameness. Respect is like art: It is hard to describe exactly, but you know it when you see it! One couple made a decision that, no matter what, they would be kind to each other. To them, this was the essence of respect—and of love.

4. Learn good communication and problem-solving skills. Love never made anyone a good mind reader. It may be tempting to believe that someone who truly loves us will magically know what we want and need, but it rarely works that way. We have already explored communication briefly (and we'll talk about it more later), but remember that you are more likely to get what you want by simply asking for it—respectfully, of course—and by recognizing that no one is obligated to give it to you! Communication skills, in and of themselves, will not create an intimate, committed relationship. Still, manipulation, game playing, and hinting around are rarely as effective as an honest discussion.

When a problem arises, do your best to work for real solutions. Be a learner, open to new ways of doing things. Mutual respect will help you find ways to compromise and discover win/win solutions. Don't forget your sense of humor; it will carry you through many tough moments.

> You are more likely to get what you want simply by asking for it—respectfully, of course—and by recognizing that no one is obligated to give it to you!

5. Take responsibility for your own choices, your own mistakes, and your own happiness. One of the biggest mistakes partners make is believing that someone else can make them happy. This is an impossible task. Happiness comes from within, and it is your responsibility. When people expect their partners to make them happy, they claim it is the partner's fault when real happiness remains elusive.

It's tempting to blame conflict, disappointment, and misunderstanding on your partner and to wait for him or her to change first. But many couples have settled into a disappointing stalemate while they wait. It is more effective to work toward self-awareness; if you are willing to own up to your own feelings and behavior, it becomes much easier for your partner to acknowledge his or hers. Change the things you can, and your partner is likely to change in response. Let go of the expectation that your partner can or should make you happy, and learn to create happiness for yourself.

6. Find help if you need it. Sorting through past decisions and the memories of childhood and past relationships can be difficult, painful work. And most couples find it extremely unnerving to tolerate the anxiety and discomfort that may be a part of growing together. You may discover that you and your partner benefit from having the support of a therapist, pastor, or support

group, and a respectful place to work on differences. A number of excellent books on personal growth and relationships are available; reading one or two with your partner may give you valuable insight and ideas.[1]

7. Invest time in your relationship. Time is like money; how you spend it reveals a great deal about your priorities. If you truly want your relationship to flourish, it will require time and attention—and there will be a lot of competition in your stepfamily for both. "Dates" and special time together will help, but you may find that holding regular "couple's meetings" gives you a way to stay in touch, identify problems before they become overwhelming, and work toward solutions.

> If you truly want your relationship to flourish, it will require time and attention—and there will be a lot of competition in your stepfamily for both.

The Couple's Meeting

YOU HAVE PROBABLY already heard of family meetings, and we will explore their usefulness for stepfamilies later in this book. But couples, too, can have meetings. In fact, regular couple's meetings can strengthen your relationship, help you solve problems, and give you frequent opportunities for laughter and fun.

---

1. Among the books we recommend on personal growth and relationships are *Passionate Marriage* (Schnarch, Owl Books, 1998), *The Seven Principles for Making Marriage Work* (Gottman and Silver, Crown, 1999), *From Here to Serenity* (Nelsen, Prima, 2000), and *Do It Yourself Therapy* (Lott, Intner, and Mendenhall, Career Press, 1999).

Here are some suggestions for conducting couple's meetings:

1. Set aside a regular time to meet as a couple—without your children. You may choose to meet in a restaurant for dinner, after the children have gone to bed, or on a weekend when they are with their other parents. Whenever you meet, be sure you make the selected time a priority. Don't let yourself be distracted by work or the telephone.

2. Begin each meeting with compliments and appreciations. Spend time during the week looking for things your partner does well, ways he or she has been helpful, or qualities that you particularly enjoy. Begin your meeting by sharing these compliments. No "buts" or "if onlys" allowed; this moment is for gratitude and appreciation only!

3. Keep an agenda board for the two of you. Put it in a place where you can easily access it. (You may want to keep it in a private place where only the two of you will see it.) When an issue or problem arises that you want to discuss with your partner, write it on the agenda. Then, at your meeting, deal with each item.

4. Brainstorm for solutions to problems. Remember that in a brainstorming session there are no bad ideas; write down each suggestion to evaluate later. Then ask yourselves, "What will happen if we do this?" When you've agreed on a solution, try it for a week or two, then check in at a future meeting to see how it is working.

5. Try the "monologue" technique. This means that one person gets to talk for at least ten minutes without interruption. It is usually best if you are sitting back to back or side by side so that body language or facial expressions don't interrupt the process. Set a timer. Some of the ten minutes may be spent in silence, but one person has the whole ten minutes. At the end of the first ten minutes, the other partner takes ten minutes, either to respond or to monologue about his or her own issues. Couples who have tried this activity report that it is amazing how often they work out their own issues during the ten minutes (or twenty if that is the agreement) just by having the chance to talk out loud without interruption.

6. End each meeting with special time for the two of you. You may want to trade back rubs, go for a walk, make a favorite dessert, or cuddle up and watch a movie.

We make time in our lives for business, volunteer work, and a host of other activities and interests; using couple's meetings to strengthen and deepen your relationship is a wise investment in the future of your stepfamily.

Putting It All Together

SIX MONTHS LATER, Neal was feeling much more hopeful about his marriage, and he was enjoying it much more. It wasn't perfect, and he realized that it probably never would be, but it was becoming better each day. He and Sharon had seen a counselor for about two months; both had learned a great deal. Neal still felt like an intruder in Sharon's home occasionally, but they had found ways to explore what the issue meant to each of them, and Sharon was working to create more space for Neal in her life—physically and emotionally.

Exploring your own feelings and experiences will help you discover whether you are ready to move forward or still need to make peace with the past.

They had created a schedule of special time together—the boys teased them mercilessly about their "dates"—and they were having regular couple's meetings. It felt a bit awkward at times, but he and Sharon both liked having a set-aside time to devote to their relationship. Neal looked forward to going home now; it actually felt like home to him. He and Sharon were even enjoying sex more—an unexpected but very pleasant bonus. Best of all, they had remembered all the reasons they got married in the first place, and they reminded each other of them frequently.

A loving, respectful relationship is one of the greatest joys you can experience in life. Living in a stepfamily presents many challenges to the couple who created it. Your family began because you and your partner found each other and decided to build a life together. Your relationship deserves your time and attention.

4

The Couple as Parents

"Who Am I, Anyway?"

Q: I am planning to marry a man with a four-year-old son. I love both of them dearly, but I do have some questions. This little boy is becoming aware of his body and is beginning to learn some naughty words. I'm wondering how to approach teaching him courtesy, kindness, and the other things he will need to know. What other concerns and frustrations do "pre-mom" candidates usually have?

A: New stepparents often find that patience and gentleness are their best friends. Many people—with the best intentions in the world—want to rush in and "parent" their stepchildren. They offer lectures, instruction, and discipline they believe is needed and are both hurt and offended when children reject their efforts or react with resistance and anger. Children must decide whether they will offer respect and trust; your stepson will do so when he is ready. Until then, you can begin by working on mutual respect, kindness, and friendship. Just hanging out, spending time together, and learning to know each other is the best parenting tool right now.

Becoming a Stepparent

IT MAY SEEM as though finding a loving, respectful partner and then building a healthy relationship are quite enough to deal with; but for most remarrying

ing couples, that is only the beginning. What comes next is what makes you a stepfamily: the children.

For most adults, beginning again with a new stepfamily means courting and being newlyweds with a curious young audience. "Between my kids living with us and his kids visiting on weekends," one woman said with a sigh, "there's never a single moment when we don't have children." Adults find themselves joining preexisting, often close-knit family groups with long-standing loyalties, traditions, and histories; fitting in can be a tricky business.

> Fitting into preexisting, close-knit family groups with long-standing loyalties, traditions, and histories can be a tricky business.

Stepparents must somehow cross the treacherous minefields of discipline and parenting styles; they must deal with children who are coping with overwhelming, sometimes unwelcome changes in their lives. Just figuring out what to call the new family members (Mom? Mary? Hey you?) can become an emotionally loaded issue. And most stepparents report that no matter how well prepared they thought they were, sooner or later they find themselves feeling overwhelmed by the complexities of stepfamily life.

Like it or not, most of those complexities have to do with the children. One survey shows that the greatest source of tension between couples who remarry is dealing with discipline. An interesting note is that this is not a problem unique to stepfamilies; virtually all couples experience some tension over the issue of discipline.

Parenting Styles: My Way or Your Way?

Q: I need help. I have an 18-year-old stepdaughter and a 15-year-old stepson. My wife and I married five years ago. We had a discussion tonight about how we managed to miss the fact that we disagree on so many issues. I told her that before we got married, she never wanted to discuss how things would be handled or what authority I would have. She said she didn't realize how much I hated her kids.

Maybe I do hate her kids. I know I dislike many of their personal habits and attitudes. I resent paying for their activities. I think they are incapable of handling anything for themselves; my wife does everything for them. My relationships with them have deteriorated to just about nothing over the past four years. Of course, this affects my relationship with my wife. I have attempted to establish some rules, but they pretty much ignore them. My wife says that I knew what I was getting myself into when I decided to marry her, but she knew my attitudes toward her kids before we got married, too. Did she think that just because we got married everything would change? I'm afraid that the older kids will affect our two-year-old daughter. Can someone help me?

A: Your discouragement echoes throughout your letter. Unfortunately; stepparents often have trouble establishing their "niche" with stepkids, especially teens, who are struggling with issues of power, individuation, and identity already. It might help to find a family therapist in your area to help you, your wife, and your kids (both step- and birth children) sort through the issues you face. For the moment, here are some things to think about.

No one but you can make you change. In the same way, you cannot *make* your wife or her children change. What usually happens is that adults change first, and those changes draw forth different reactions from kids—eventually. Your stepchildren can easily see the difference in the way you feel towards your two-year-old and them, and, being human, it hurts them. They translate their discouragement into anger, defiance, and other annoying behavior, such as ignoring your rules. After all, if not for you they'd have their mom all to themselves.

It's important to note that treating kids "the same" is rarely possible, nor is feeling "the same" about them. But "the same" is not an issue when everyone knows he or she will be treated with respect and kindness. Hating your stepchildren will only do damage to them, to you, and to your wife. But there is no law that says you have to like them, either. You can dislike their personalities and attitudes and still choose to treat them with courtesy and respect, thus modeling the behavior you expect from them.

> The most effective parenting style balances firmness with flexibility and kindness.

As much as possible, make discipline decisions *with* your wife, and present them to all three kids as a team. If you're making the rules and enforcing them while your wife "does everything" for the kids, you're the natural target of their defiance (and all teens have some). Your stepchildren need to learn responsibility and the life skills they will need to live successful lives, and you and your wife need to back each other up.

Perhaps most important, remember that everyone in your family wants to have a feeling of belonging and significance, something that can be especially difficult in stepfamilies, in which everything seems to have changed. Your stepchildren's behavior is their way of letting you and their mom know they don't feel they belong or are important, and they have found unpleasant but effective ways of creating their own sense of power. Finding ways they can belong and contribute will help change the atmosphere. Real change takes time: until it happens, you may have to "fake it 'til you make it."

How Do We Parent Together When We Don't Agree?

YOU MAY HAVE heard that opposites attract. One of the ways couples are "opposite" is their individual approach to parenting—their parenting style. Remarrying parents often do not become aware that they approach parenting in different ways until they—and all their children—are living together under one roof. Usually one spouse leans slightly toward permissiveness, while the other leans toward strictness or control. When their styles clash (and they inevitably do), parents usually go to extremes. The slightly permissive parent becomes excessively so to compensate for the "mean," strict parent. The strict parent becomes excessively controlling to make up for that "wishy-washy," lenient parent. Then they fight about who is right and who is wrong.

The truth is that children benefit from neither excessive control nor excessive permissiveness. Moreover, disagreements between parents often invite manipulation from the children, who quickly learn to pit one against the other to get what they want.

As we will see, the most effective parenting style balances firmness with flexibility and kindness. Children do best when parents respect each other's different styles. The good news is that children can learn to adapt their behavior to the parent they are dealing with. The really good news is that the whole family can work together to find solutions and mutually beneficial agreements when "right" and "wrong" are no longer the issue. The key is mutual respect, a main topic in parenting classes (which are a source of many examples presented in this book). Parents and their partners may find it is well worth the investment of time and money to find a good parenting class to help them blend their parenting styles as well as their families.

Differing parenting styles can be a problem in any family, but stepparents are expected to perform a difficult job for which they receive little recognition and no instruction. We celebrate Mother's Day and Father's Day, but what about Stepparents' Day? (Yes, there actually is one—September 16—but how many people are aware of it?) How often are children in school offered the opportunity and materials to make a gift for their parents and stepparents?

Gather together a roomful of stepparents, and you'll hear several questions over and over. Should I discipline the kids or should I let their "real" parent do that? Who should be most important—my kids or my spouse? Do I have to treat his kids the same as I treat mine? Should I feel the same way about her children as I do my own kids? What if I don't love my stepchildren? What if the grandparents favor their biological grandchildren over their step-grandchildren? Every time I ask my stepdaughter to do something, she complains to her dad—and he always takes her side. What should I do about that? Is it wrong for me to want time alone with my wife, without her children? How will I ever fit into this family, anyway?

It probably can't be said too often: Learning to live together as a stepfamily, to sort out roles and responsibilities, and to build new relationships takes patience, commitment, and time. In case you're wondering, it *is* possible. How do stepparents figure out where they fit and what to do?

"Who Am I, Anyway?"

SANDY COLLAPSED INTO a chair in her parenting class. "I'm so tired," she said, running her fingers through her hair. "I never thought taking care of a child could be so much work!"

Ann, the parenting class leader, smiled sympathetically. "What's going on, Sandy?"

Sandy looked at her husband and drew a long, slow breath. "Well, Rick and I have been married for eight months now. We're really happy—most of the time—but his little girl, Megan, is a handful. She's four, and she never slows down. She spends one week with us and one week with her mom. Rick works evenings, so I end up taking care of Megan. Rick and I agreed that he would be in charge of disciplining her, but he's never around! When I try to correct her or put her to bed, she has a tantrum and screams for her dad. We get along fine as long as I do everything she wants.

"There's another problem, too. I want Megan and me to have a real relationship. After all, we're going to be part of each other's lives for a long time. I want to be special to Megan, but I don't want to try to replace her mother. Megan really loves her mom. She misses her when she's with us, and I think she takes that out on me sometimes. We haven't even figured out what Megan should call me. Her mother feels hurt if she calls me 'Mom,' but 'Sandy' sounds disrespectful to me. I'm worn out and grumpy; when Rick comes home, we end up arguing about Megan. I don't know what to do."

"Well, taking a parenting class together is a good beginning," Ann said. "Has anyone else here ever felt the way Sandy does?" Sandy gave a weary smile as hands went up around the room.

"I guess I'm not alone," she said, "but I'm not sure that makes it any easier."

Defining Roles and Responsibilities

As we've said before, stepfamilies can be complicated. So many variables are possible that deciding how yours should function can be difficult. The roles adults play in a stepfamily will vary depending on who is in the family. Do both adults have children? Only one? How much parenting experience do the adults have? How much time do the children spend in the home?

Women sometimes have a more difficult time adjusting to being stepparents, possibly because our culture traditionally has taught us that women have primary responsibility for creating and maintaining a home and nurturing the people who live there. Women may want more love and connection, feel more vulnerable, and put more pressure on themselves to be "good" stepparents than men do. They may expect more of themselves—and have more expected of them by their partners. But no one is born instinctively knowing how to be a good stepmother; most women find they must learn new skills and ease into their new role gradually.

Because mothers often have primary custody of children, stepfathers frequently find themselves living with their stepchildren, and they may feel guilty about spending time with them or be reluctant to grow close or be involved in parenting. After all, shouldn't a father devote that time to his own children? Divorce and the reorganization of families put a great deal of pressure on men. How can they stay connected to their birth children when those children live in another home (or city, or state)? Where do they fit in their stepchildren's lives? What is a father's role, anyway?

> No one knows instinctively how to be a good stepparent; most people find they must learn new skills and ease into their new role gradually.

Our culture has traditionally expected that fathers will take charge of discipline in the home. (How many children have grown up with mothers who say, "Wait 'til your father gets home!"?) Many well-meaning stepfathers create tension and resentment by trying to assume a role of authority too soon, before children (and their partners) have had time to welcome their involvement. Both partners may find it easy to idealize their own children's behavior while finding fault with the behavior of their partner's children. Mutual respect and fairness are admirable goals, but they don't happen overnight. How do we find our way?

As with any journey, it helps to know where you're going as you decide how your stepfamily should work. Remember the things you said you wanted for your family? Those ideals and qualities are your destination; deciding on roles and responsibilities will depend on your own individual decisions about what is most important for you, your partner, and your family. The following suggestions may help you make some of these important decisions.

1. Recognize that many roles are available. If your stepchildren's birth parent is no longer an active part of their lives, they may be excited and eager to accept you as a "real" parent. If they spend time with their birth parent, especially if they love and miss him or her, it may take you some time to find a space in their lives as their "other" mother or father that fits for both of you.

BECOMING A STEPPARENT: HOW DO YOU BEGIN?

1. Recognize that many roles are available.

2. Try to build a united front.

3. Understand the true meaning of discipline.

4. Spend "special time" with each child.

5. Educate yourself about child development.

6. Be involved when possible.

7. Work toward respect and courtesy rather than expecting love.

8. Avoid comparing children.

9. Don't take things personally.

It can be helpful to acknowledge that you are a newcomer in your step-children's lives and to ask them for their ideas about how you can be most helpful. Many children welcome a friend, mentor, and confidante but resist a would-be parent. Country singer Reba McEntire once shared on a talk show that she enjoys being a stepparent. In the beginning, she told her stepchildren, "I'm not your mama. I want to be your friend."

One stepmother found that by listening respectfully to her teenaged step-daughter, she was able to offer help and ideas without getting drawn into conflicts between the girl and her birth parents. It is usually wise to let children set the pace, even if you wish things could be different. Be open and available, but avoid pushing. Real trust and respect happen one step at a time.

2. Try to build a united front. No two parents—whether they're first-timers or stepparents—will consistently agree on all aspects of parenting. You and your partner may have very different ideas about the best way to raise your children. In addition, for better or worse, children are amazingly perceptive; they notice those differences and use them to their own advantage.

Taking time to learn more about parenting and to decide what works best for you and your family is a wonderful investment in your future together. Reading this book is a good first step; taking a parenting class together might be another. Decide what you will do, and follow through with dignity and respect.

When conflict or unforeseen problems arise (as they almost always do), use your couple's meetings to find solutions. It usually works best to support each other in the children's presence and work out differences in private. Let your children see that you and your partner love one another, consult with one another, and support one another. It will help you avoid manipulation and competition.

When one parent will have most of the child care responsibilities, that parent must have the ability and respect to parent effectively. Using family meetings to build relationships and work for solutions together will help immensely (more on family meetings later).

Presenting a united family front with grandparents, who may struggle with new family additions, is important. It may help to let the children's grandparents know that while you don't expect them to love their step-grandchildren as much as they love their own, you do expect that all of your children will be treated with dignity and respect. Some stepfamilies decide not to visit grandparents who show blatant favoritism because they are unwilling to expose their children to that kind of rejection. The following suggestions will help prevent feelings of rejection for children in most situations.

> It can be helpful to acknowledge that you are a newcomer in your stepchildren's lives and to ask them for their ideas about how you can be most helpful.

3. Understand the true meaning of discipline. Almost all stepparents have asked the question, "Who should discipline the children?" When you understand that discipline and punishment are not the same, you will eliminate the issue of who should be the disciplinarian. Of course a stepparent can "discipline" his or her stepchildren when the discipline is nonpunitive, respectful, and designed to teach life skills. Throughout this book we will provide many disciplinary methods that are much more effective than any kind of punishment.

Many parents don't realize that sometimes the best form of discipline is simply to spend time with children. "A misbehaving child is a discouraged child" (Dreikurs), and encouragement is the best way to help children change their behavior in positive ways. A major cause of discouragement is a feeling of not belonging. Thus spending time with a child can help him or her feel a sense of belonging and encouragement—thus eliminating the need to misbehave.

4. Spend "special time" with each child. "I hardly know my stepmother," one 11-year-old girl said. "When I go to my dad's house, she says 'hi,' but then she ignores me. She's really busy with her two kids—they have lots of activities to go to. I feel left out and unimportant. I love my dad, but it's hard to visit him when I feel so rejected by my stepmother."

We are not suggesting that you must love your stepchildren as much as your own. However, it is common courtesy to be aware of their feelings and to treat them with respect. It is hard for a relationship—whether friendship or something deeper—to happen if you spend little time with the people who share your life. All human beings feel the need to belong; when they don't feel a sense of being wanted and valued, problems often arise. Although it may feel awkward at first, spending "special time" with each child in your stepfamily creates an atmosphere of curiosity and interest in which real connection can flourish.

Set aside time regularly (at least once each week works well for many families) to spend with each child, whether your own or your partner's. This time need not be long, nor must it involve expensive activities. Sometimes reading a story aloud

> To avoid manipulation and competition, let your children see that you and your partner love one another, consult with one another, and support one another.

together, going for a walk, inviting a child to help you with a task, or having a conversation between "just the two of you" may be enough. If other children in the family protest, remind them that they, too, will have their turn. Special time can be scheduled in advance, or it may happen spontaneously, just as long as it happens!

> Spending "special time" with each child creates an atmosphere of curiosity and interest in which real connection can flourish.

5. Educate yourself about child development. Many stepparents have no children of their own and find "instant parenthood" confusing and frustrating. Many of these parents, who have every intention of loving their stepchildren, fail to understand those children's behavior. If you have no prior experience with children (and sometimes even if you do!), make an effort to educate yourself about your children's emotional, mental, and physical development and how their ages and stages affect their behavior. A little bit of knowledge about developmentally appropriate behavior—and how to manage it—can save all of you a great deal of misunderstanding and conflict.

6. Be involved when possible. Make an effort to attend school, athletic, and other events your stepchildren are involved in, and invite your partner to attend your children's activities. Just being there shows genuine interest, and children notice and appreciate when we take time to be involved in their lives.

Remember to respect children's need for time with their own parent as well. Try not to take it personally if your stepchildren ask for time with mom or dad without you. Knowing when your presence is wanted and when it is not can take a great deal of sensitivity and patience. Listen—to your partner, the children, and your inner wisdom—and you will usually know. If you're not good at reading minds (and who is?), you might simply ask children whether they would like you to be present for activities (and, perhaps, how they wish you to be introduced). If you meet with resistance, be patient; look for moments when you can offer a compliment or a smile. Change that lasts usually begins with small steps.

7. Work toward respect and courtesy rather than expecting love. Children will not automatically love a stepparent—and stepparents will not automatically love their stepchildren. Sometimes, as Sandy discovered with Megan, just keeping the peace can be a challenge!

If you are fortunate enough to feel genuine affection for your stepchildren and to have that feeling returned, celebrate daily! If you and your stepchildren are still working toward a close, trusting relationship, have faith that offering courtesy and respect—important ingredients in love—is an excellent beginning.

"My stepkids barely tolerate me," some adults may think. "Why should I respect them? Shouldn't they respect me first?" Children learn respect by seeing what it looks like; adults must respect themselves and each other, and offer respect to children. This may be as simple as being calm and courteous. There is a huge difference between what we feel

> Remember to respect children's need for time with their own parent as well.

and what we do. Even when you don't yet feel love or affection for your stepchildren, you can choose to act in ways that demonstrate respect. Again, although it may not seem fair, adults usually must change first; children change in response.

8. Avoid comparing children. This tip is easier said than done. It is normal for adults to compare their own children with those of relatives, friends, neighbors—and new spouses. Bill's 19-year-old stepson, Greg, is an impressive young man: intelligent, hardworking, ambitious—and he managed to earn and save most of the tuition money for his first year of college. But when Bill says to Brandon, his own son, "Why can't you be more like Greg? You spend every penny you get as soon as it hits your palm," he is forgetting that Brandon is seven years younger and has a different set of life experiences. Now Brandon feels put down; it's easy for him to believe his dad loves him less than he loves Greg. And those feelings may lead to behavior his dad finds even less acceptable.

Comparing children is like comparing apples and oranges; although both are fruit, they are very different! If blending your families points out areas where children could improve, then concentrate on using encouragement and teaching to bring about change. Once again, working toward trust and respect will set the foundation on which to build positive changes in behavior.

9. Don't take things personally. Adjusting to a new family can be especially difficult for children who don't have the maturity and wisdom to understand their emotions and how to deal with change. (Unfortunately, this also describes many adults.) Children who feel discouraged (who lack the feelings of belonging and significance) may take it out on everyone near them. A stepparent makes an excellent target.

Five-year-old Melissa's biological mom abandoned her when she was only two years old. She pops in and out of Melissa's life once in a while, but she is not a nurturing mother. Melissa's new stepmother, Janice, is very nurturing and caring. She wants very much to help Melissa feel loved and special. Melissa, however, acts as though she is desperate to gain her biological mother's love. No matter what Janice does, Melissa says, "My mom doesn't do it that way."

When Janice brought this concern to her parenting class, tears came to her eyes as she shared how hurt she felt. She described a time when she was brushing Melissa's hair and Melissa said, "Ouch, you pulled my hair. My mommy doesn't do that." Janice retorted that her mommy didn't take care of her grooming at all.

During the "brainstorming for solutions time," the group came up with many suggestions for Janice to try. The one she liked best was to avoid getting hooked into taking it personally by giving Melissa a hug and ignoring the criticism. Janice received a lot of validation from the group about how lucky Melissa was to have Janice in her life, even if Melissa could not yet comprehend that because she still felt abandoned by her mother.

At the next class, Janice was beaming. She reported that responding to the criticism with a hug changed her own attitude so much that it couldn't help but affect Melissa. Melissa seemed surprised at first, then nuzzled into the hug. Janice came up with a brilliant addition to the suggestion she was following. After the hug, she said to Melissa, "Would you like to get your doll and brush her hair while I brush yours? We could both try our best not to pull while we brush out the knots." Melissa did not complain about the slight pulls to her hair as she and Janice finished the job together.

There is lots of room in a child's life for love, affection, and respect; there is no limit to the number of adults who can provide these precious qualities. Finding your special place in your stepchildren's lives may take some time. Practice patience, be content with small beginnings, and work with your partner to learn effective parenting skills.

Sandy and Rick's parenting group helped them understand the importance of supporting each other with Megan, as well as learn the skills to set boundaries and understand the behavior of an active four-year-old. Sandy decided to spend some special time each day just having fun with her stepdaughter. She also gave up her expectation that an intimate, loving relationship would happen quickly and decided to focus on mutual respect instead. Janice's parenting group helped her recognize her own efforts and shift her focus to meeting Melissa's needs, rather than getting hooked into the criticism by taking it personally.

Does Equal Have to Mean the Same?

EVERYTHING IN A stepfamily, from money to closet space to food, can seem to have hidden meaning. Why does Jimmy get his own room when I have to share? Why do my stepdad's kids get to have art lessons and I can't? Why do I have to do more chores than my stepsister? Who is most important? Which of us do you love the most?

Adults usually want to keep everything fair and even, and it often becomes an astonishingly difficult (if not impossible) task. You probably feel drawn to your own children—after all, you've known them longer and shared more with them. Then, because you believe you should be able to treat everyone equally, you may feel guilty.

> There is lots of room in a child's life for love, affection, and respect; there is no limit to the number of adults who can provide these precious qualities.

What is equal, anyway? Is it wrong to favor your own children over your partner's? Is it possible not to? Each member of a stepfamily has his or her own unique perspective, needs, and desires. Also, "equal" does not necessarily mean "the same."

Remember, what you feel and what you choose to do are separate things. Use family meetings to communicate, share ideas and opinions respectfully, and look for solutions. When children are part of the brainstorming for solutions to problems (such as getting the chores done), they feel equal in their opportunity to give suggestions and in the decision-making process. Also, when children help create the solutions, they are more likely to abide by them.

Try for balance rather than equality, and involve children in the process of finding it. Compromise and negotiation are valuable skills. Life is not always "fair"— but listening well and helping each family member experience a sense of belonging, a feeling of significance, and positive ways to contribute to the new family will make life easier.

> Listening well and helping each family member experience a sense of belonging, a feeling of significance, and positive ways to contribute to the new family will make life easier.

George (the father of two teenaged sons) and Martha (the mother of two teenaged daughters) decided to get married. They had courted for over a year, and their children liked each other. Still, they were concerned. Their children were used to having their own rooms, but they would be moving into a four-bedroom house. Two of the children would have to share a room.

George and Martha were worried about how to solve this dilemma. Should the boys or girls share a room? How would they decide? Would the teens who had to share a room feel angry or resentful?

In desperation, George and Martha decided to involve the kids and ask for their opinions. They were amazed at how quickly their children solved the problem. The boys "offered" to share a room because, as they said, "The girls have more junk and need more room."

It is our guess that these young people might have felt resentment if their parents had made the decision without respectfully involving the children. Asking their opinion invited their cooperation.

The Courage to Be Imperfect

EVEN WITH ALL the best intentions in the world and armed with excellent advice, we will inevitably make mistakes. This new family is unfamiliar territory for all of us, and both adults and children will need some time to find their way around.

Rudolf Dreikurs spoke often about the "courage to be imperfect." It does indeed take courage to tackle a new role in a new family when you know in advance that you will make mistakes. Still, mistakes aren't fatal, and neither are hurt feelings. You can survive them and even grow stronger because of them if you can remember that mistakes are opportunities to learn. Ironically, trust and closeness often grow through the process of recognizing mistakes, apologizing for them, and working together to make things right.

> Trust and closeness often grow through the process of recognizing mistakes, apologizing for them, and working together to make things right.

If you've made mistakes in dealing with your stepchildren, your own children, or your partner, take a deep breath and dust yourself off. Ask yourself what would work better next time, invite help from those around you, and try again. You and those you love are worth it!

5

Enter the Children

LISA WAS NINE years old when her mother married Dan. She had never
known her own father; he had left Lisa and her mother, Christy, when Lisa
was just a baby. Christy had worked hard to make a comfortable home for
them. She had often been weary, anxious, and lonely, and mother and daughter were both happy when Dan came into their lives. Finally, Lisa and her
beloved mom would have someone to take care of them. Dan had two daughters of his own, twins named Kate and Maggie, and Lisa was genuinely thrilled
with the idea of having not only a dad but also real "big sisters."

As so often happens, though, reality turned out to be more complicated
than anyone had expected. Lisa had always wanted a brother or sister, but suddenly she discovered that being an only child had distinct advantages. Lisa and
Christy had always been close; both had looked forward to the end of each day
when they could be together and share news about work and school. Now Lisa
had to share her mother with Dan. They were always going into the bedroom
together or having whispered conversations when they thought Lisa wasn't
paying attention.

As if that wasn't bad enough, when Kate and Maggie came to stay
(Wednesday nights and every other weekend), Lisa wasn't the only child at all;
she was the baby, and she didn't like it one bit! Kate and Maggie got more privileges than Lisa did—they were older. Somehow they had fewer chores to do
because they weren't around as often as Lisa was. And being twins seemed to

make them special; they got lots of attention, dressed in special ways, and always had each other for company.

Lisa's feelings were hurt, and when her hurt feelings weren't recognized, she became sulky. Pouting got her noticed, all right, but not in a helpful way. Dan called her "sullen" and began avoiding her; Christy worried that her daughter's behavior would doom her new marriage and began to nag and lecture Lisa.

> For better or worse, children's feelings are almost always reflected in their behavior.

One night, during an argument with her mother about her attitude, Lisa blew up. "I hate being in this family," she said with passionate tears in her eyes. "I wish you'd never met Dan. I wish it could be just us again. You love everyone else more than me!" Lisa fled to her room, slamming the door and leaving her exasperated mother to wonder what had happened to the dreams of family harmony.

The children of stepfamilies are almost always children of loss. They are entering a new family because something in their first family didn't work out right; a parent left or died, or their mom and dad divorced. Adults entering stepfamilies may feel apprehensive, but they usually are excited and hopeful as well. Children's emotions are often far more complicated, and expressing and dealing with their emotions are far harder for children than for adults. And for better or worse, children's feelings are almost always reflected in their behavior.

Children have little power to choose what happens in their families. They are seldom consulted if their parents divorce; they do not make the decision about whom they will live with (unless they are teenagers) or visitation schedules. They aren't usually asked whether they would like to move to another neighborhood, go to a different school, or share their room with a new sibling.

If children move between Mom's house and Dad's house (and many, many children do exactly that these days), they are expected to adjust to different rules, family roles, and lifestyles. Sometimes just getting homework assignments turned in becomes a logistical nightmare (the report is due tomorrow and the encyclopedia is at Dad's!).

Even when the decision to remarry was a good one and both adults are working hard to establish trust, respect, and stability, children still must resolve a number of tricky emotional issues. This

> Understanding your children's percep-tions about their situa-tion will help you deal with their behavior and focus on solutions that nurture closeness and trust.

does not mean that creating your stepfamily was a mistake; it does mean that good communication and problem-solving skills are vital, along with a healthy dose of patience and empathy. Understanding your children's perceptions about their situation will help you deal with their behavior and to focus on solutions that nurture closeness and trust.

The Importance of Belonging

IF YOU ASK adults what children need most to be healthy and happy, they usually will say love. Love is certainly important, but it is not the entire answer. What children (and all the rest of us) need to be healthy and happy is a sense of belonging and significance. We each need to believe we fit in and are wanted and needed simply for who we are. We each need to be able to make a contribution and to feel that our presence has value.

When a person doesn't feel that she belongs, she may try to create that feeling in other ways—often with self-defeating behavior. We'll look closely at the mistaken goals of behavior and how to deal with them later on, but for now, consider that belonging begins in the family. For children, being part of a step-family may call that sense of belonging into question.

Think for a moment about your own children. Put yourself into their small shoes. What does it feel like to be them? How have their lives changed? Even positive changes may take getting used to, and some children don't welcome the changes in their lives at all! Children in stepfamilies have a number of issues in common. Understanding these can help you see beyond children's behavior and into their hearts.

Changes in Birth Order

IT'S BEEN SAID before that every child is born into a different family. Each child's position in the family—his birth order—has a great deal to do with how he sees himself and where he fits in his family. As we discussed in chapter 3, children make decisions about themselves based on how they perceive the world. One basic issue that is influenced by birth order is "What do I need to do to belong in this family and to feel significant?" Oldest children often decide, "I belong only if I'm first or best." How do they come to this conclusion?

Firstborn children are often treated as the "best" child that was ever born. They live in a world populated by adults. They often acquire language quickly and are more articulate than children born later. Oldest children often have more privileges in the family—but much is expected of them, too. How many oldest children have heard the words, "Share with your little brother! You're the oldest—you should know better!"

Some oldest children become perfectionists, always trying to do things right. Others succeed in their quest for excellence and become high achievers. Sometimes oldest children feel so pressured to live up to expectations that they give up instead. They believe, "If I can't be best or first, I won't even try." It is important to note that there are as many exceptions to rules about birth order as there are generalizations. The point is to understand how birth order might affect each child's decisions about who she is and what she needs to do to find a sense of belonging and significance.

Youngest children are the "babies." One fourth grader, a proud youngest child, said, "We get the most toys and stuff!" Youngest children often find that the rules have been relaxed a bit by the time they come along; parents have practiced on the older children and have learned to lighten up. Their siblings, however, frequently perceive youngest children as spoiled—and often they are! Many youngest children decide, "I belong and am significant only when others take care of me." These children often develop manipulation skills that are irresistible and with which they charm others into taking care of them. Other youngest children tire of being last in line for the privileges of growing up and become "speeders." They decide, "I will feel a sense of belonging and significance only when I do as well as (or even better than) my siblings." These decisions are made subconsciously, and children usually are not aware of them; however, if you watch closely, you can see them being played out in a child's life.

Middle children sometimes feel lost in the family shuffle and turn to peers and siblings for support and encouragement. One researcher found that middle children often have the fewest pictures in their family albums. They may choose a piece of the family pie that is distinctly different from the children who have come before. If the oldest child is interested in music, the next-born may prefer gymnastics; that way, she doesn't have to compete for a slice of the pie that is already taken. Middle children often feel "squeezed." They don't have the privileges of the oldest or the special treatment of the youngest. They may feel they are treated unfairly. Because they understand how underdogs feel, they often become "champions of the underdog." They may decide that they will feel a sense of belonging and significance in the world through some kind of social work, by bringing justice to the world. Some middle children become rebels (with or without a cause) in their attempt to find belonging and significance; many decide to look for a sense of belonging with their peers rather than their families.

> Blending families together usually scrambles the birth-order arrangements, and children sometimes have difficulty adjusting.

Only children have their own unique situation as the recipient of their parents' undivided attention. They are often highly motivated, sometimes lonely, and occasionally slow at learning to share and be flexible (although they sometimes have an easier time sharing because they did not "have" to share before they were ready). They may also learn to be more comfortable with "alone time" than other children.

While birth order is certainly not a reliable predictor of a child's abilities or behavior, it does affect the way children see themselves and the way they define where they belong in their families. Why is it important to consider birth order? Blending families together usually scrambles the birth-order arrangements, and children sometimes have difficulty adjusting. An oldest child may suddenly become a middle or a youngest. She was once "dethroned" as the only child by the birth of younger siblings and now is "dethroned" all over again as the oldest. This requires a lot of adjustment in the subconscious mind, where conclusions have already been reached about how to find belonging and significance.

To further complicate matters, many children have one position at Mom's house and another at Dad's. James, for instance, is the oldest child at his mother's house. He helps take care of his little brother and gets to stay up half an hour later. At his father's house, though, he's right in the middle of five children and has to go to bed with everyone else. Is it any wonder that children sometimes feel confused about what is expected of them and by whom?

> Stepsiblings can learn to get along together, but they will almost certainly need adult help and encouragement.

Lisa, whom we met earlier, was used to being the only child of a single mother. They were a tightly knit little family, and Lisa received a great deal of attention from her mom. When Christy married Dan, Lisa became the youngest of three girls and resented the loss of her exclusive position. This does not mean she is spoiled or selfish; it does mean that her world has changed and, along with it, her perception of whether (and where) she belongs. When Christy and Dan can understand this and create ways for all three girls to find belonging and significance, it is likely that Lisa's "attitude problems" will improve.

Becoming a stepfamily introduces many huge changes. Adults can help children cope (and even thrive) if they have a compassionate understanding of their world and can help them sort out their feelings and work for solutions to the problems that arise.

Acquiring—and Living with—Stepsiblings

BLENDING FAMILIES OFTEN means that a child acquires not only a new stepparent; he or she may also acquire one or more siblings. Having new brothers or sisters can be fun for a child, but it can also feel strange and unsettling. Small things can suddenly have a great deal of importance: Who gets to have a room to himself? Whose favorite snack foods will we buy? Who has more privileges? More of Mom's time? Who always whines and gets her way?

Adding new children to a family has undeniable effects on everyone. Space and privacy are often in short supply, as are parental time and attention. It's not unusual for stepsiblings to resent each other and to feel compelled to compete with one another, and there are no biological ties to encourage them to work things out. In even the happiest of birth families, siblings bicker to attract their parents' attention; in stepfamilies, children unsure of where they fit often resort to arguing to test their parent's (and stepparent's) reactions.

Adjusting to life in a stepfamily may be even more complicated when some of the children involved only visit. Custody and visitation agreements often give children only weekends or vacations with one parent. When children go to visit Dad and find their stepmother's children in comfortable permanent residence, what are they to do? How can they feel belonging and significance when no one is sure where they belong?

It can help adults keep their perspective to remember that all children occasionally disagree, compete with one another, and fight. Because family life rarely resembles a Norman Rockwell painting for long, expecting utter and total peace, harmony, and tranquility is unrealistic.

Stepsiblings can learn to get along together, but they will almost certainly need adult help and encouragement. You will find lots of suggestions for creating unity and harmony in your stepfamily in the chapters that follow, but here are a few ideas to consider now:

1. Maintain a united front. (Yes, it works here, too.) It can be helpful to let children know that you and your partner intend for this family to endure

KEEPING THE PEACE: HELPING STEPSIBLINGS GET ALONG

1. Maintain a united front.

2. Don't expect instant affection and trust among children.

3. Validate feelings.

4. Help each child find a place to belong and feel significant.

5. Have regular family meetings.

6. Allow children room to be themselves.

7. Don't play "referee."

8. Keep schools informed.

9. Be patient.

and that you will work together to make it happen. It may take time, but children can learn to accept that things have changed—and that there may be advantages to their new family once everyone settles in.

2. Don't expect instant affection and trust among children. Just as stepparents and stepchildren will not automatically love each other, stepsiblings also will not form instant bonds of affection and trust. Help children find ways to explore and express their feelings; concentrate on courtesy and mutual respect. Courtesy and respect will not magically lead to sibling love, but peace depends on these ingredients.

3. Validate feelings. Many parents try to talk children out of their feelings. "Don't be silly. I love you just as much," or "That is a selfish way to feel." This only increases a child's discouragement. On the other hand, a child can feel very encouraged just by hearing, "I can see that this is very hard for you and that you feel unloved right now," or "It can be very hard to share me with others when you have never had to do that before." It is very helpful to teach children that feelings are never right or wrong—they are just feelings, and they are valid. As we pointed out before, there is a big difference between what children feel and what they do. After feelings have been validated, children may be willing to work toward solutions to the problems that inspired the feelings. And, as in so many other aspects of family life, as time passes and everyone feels more comfortable, feelings that are acknowledged and understood often resolve themselves.

4. Help each child find a place to belong and feel significant. You can help each child in your family create some personal space. Even if children must share rooms, private corners and study spaces can be built, personal property respected, and time allowed for each child to be alone. Having even a small space that is "mine" can help children adjust more quickly to the things that must be shared.

5. Have regular family meetings. Use these meetings to share compliments, have fun, and solve problems together in mutually respectful ways. Be open to hearing each child's perception of what is happening; sometimes minor adjustments to routines and chores can make life feel more "fair" to all concerned. Remember, too, that it isn't always possible to be totally fair; listen calmly, invite suggestions and solutions, and do the best you can.

> Having even a small space that is "mine" can help children adjust more quickly to the things that must be shared.

6. Allow children room to be themselves. It is tempting to expect your stepchildren to behave like your own children, to share their interests, and to react in similar ways—and life would almost certainly be simpler if they did! Each child in your family, however, is an individual. Look for and encourage their strengths and unique qualities; it will not only help them feel and behave their best but it will also strengthen your growing relationship with each child and lessen their need to compete with each other.

7. Don't play "referee." Teach children problem-solving and conflict resolution skills, then invite them to work out their own problems. Create a family slogan, such as "We are not looking for blame; we are looking for solutions." Arguing and fighting among siblings (and stepsiblings) are often related to adult attention. Putting children in the same boat (not taking sides) can prevent perceptions of favoritism. One way to put children in the same boat is to say, "I have faith that you kids can figure out a solution to this problem. Let me know when you have found a win/win solution."

8. Keep schools informed. Teachers, principals, and counselors can be wonderful allies in your efforts to create a healthy family. Stepsiblings sometimes wind up in the same schools (and even the same classes); occasional talks with the teacher may keep tension at home from spilling over to the school setting. Invite children to sit in on parent-teacher conferences and suggest ways they can help each other learn and grow—at home and at school.

9. Be patient. We'll say it again: Be patient. Even children who genuinely like each other argue sometimes. A real relationship takes time.

When Children Grieve: Understanding the Impact of Loss

AS WE HAVE noted before, children in stepfamilies usually have suffered losses of some sort. One parent may have died, or they may have endured the separation of their parents and the breakup of their family's home. They may be hoping their birth parents will get back together and be unwilling to accept their new stepfamily; they may be mourning the loss of old friends, old neighbors, their old room, or old traditions. Like adults, children who have experienced a loss feel intense grief, but they express grief in very different ways than adults. Because they still think in very concrete, black-and-white ways, children who grieve often engage in "magical thinking," believing, "If I hadn't acted that way, Daddy wouldn't have left," or "If I'm good, Mommy and Daddy will get back together." Or children may not express their grief at all; they may bury it in an attempt to get along or to protect their parents. Unexpressed grief goes underground where it silently influences the way a child feels, thinks, and acts.

> Children often can accept new step-parents and siblings more easily when they realize that enjoying their new family does not mean forgetting their past.

Grief and depression in children can be easily mistaken for other problems. Grieving children may become irritable, hyperactive, or aggressive; their eating and sleeping patterns may change; their behavior may regress to an earlier stage; or they may struggle to do their schoolwork or get along with their siblings and friends. In fact, some recent research indicates that unresolved grief in children may mimic the symptoms of attention deficit disorder. How many of the vast numbers of children diagnosed with ADD might actually be wrestling with grief or depression instead?

Unfortunately, children usually experience grief at a time when adults are least able to offer support and understanding. Adults coping with death, divorce, or abandonment experience their own depression and sorrow; they may recognize that their children have strong feelings, too, but be unable to set aside their own emotions to help their children. Or they may believe their children are simply "acting out" and respond with punishment or lectures.

Grief is a uniquely personal emotion; you may not think the children in your family have any reason to feel it, but that does not mean they do not. If your own children or those of your partner have experienced death, divorce, or abandonment by parents, even if it happened some time ago, you may be wise to consider the possibility that they are grieving and will require your support to adjust to their new family. We will learn more about feelings and communication skills in chapter 8, but recognizing children's grief and gently inviting them to explore and, eventually, resolve these feelings can help them deal with the changes in their lives. Children often can accept new stepparents and siblings more easily when they realize that enjoying their new family does not mean forgetting their past.

What If There's an "Ours"? Should We Have a Baby?

SOONER OR LATER, many remarried couples consider having a child of their own, an "ours" to go with the "yours" and/or "mine" they already have. Couples often wonder what effect a new baby will have on their stepfamily. Will it make the family stronger? Or will it cause new problems? There's no easy answer to these questions. A new addition to the family may create some resentment among children, but it can also provide an opportunity to teach valuable lessons about love, belonging, and what it means to be a family.

"Honey, what time is the boys' basketball practice?" Mark called. He walked into the bathroom to find Rhonda sitting on the edge of the bathtub with a dazed expression on her face. "What is it, Rhonda? Are you okay?" he asked.

Rhonda looked up at him and mutely handed over the home pregnancy test.

"What's this?" Mark asked. Then, after he looked more closely, he dropped down onto the tub next to his wife. "You're pregnant?"

Rhonda nodded and sighed. "I guess so. Oh, Mark, what will happen now? We've talked about having a baby, but I'm afraid this is too soon. The boys still don't seem happy about us being together. What if they resent the baby?"

Mark put an arm around his wife and smiled at her. "I'm sure we can work it out, honey. And I'm glad you're pregnant. I love you, you know." Mark pulled Rhonda to her feet and enveloped her in a hug.

Rhonda and Mark waited a while to break the news to the boys. Carl, eight, and Jake, five, had struggled with their mom's decision to marry Mark. They had never given up hope that she and their dad would get back together, and they had resisted spending time with Mark, resented his attempts to be involved in their lives and to discipline them, and sulked when their mom spent time with her new husband. They fought often with each other, with their mom, and with Mark—and they weren't exactly thrilled with the news.

"You're going to have a *baby*?" Carl said. "Why? Aren't Jake and I enough?"

"We don't need any babies around here," Jake chimed in.

Rhonda took a deep breath and smiled at her sons. "Come here, guys," she said. "I want to tell you a story about our family."

Carl and Jake reluctantly sat down next to their mother on the sofa and watched as she lit a tall blue candle. "This candle is me," she said, "and this flame represents my love. A long time ago, I got news just like this—except that time, Carl, it was you." Rhonda picked up a smaller purple candle and lit it with the flame from her tall one. "When you were born, I gave you all my love, but I still had all my love left. Then, three years later, I got news like this again."

"It was me!" Jake shouted out.

Rhonda laughed. "It sure was." She picked up a small, yellow candle and lit it with the flame from her blue one. "And when you were born, I gave you all my love. Carl still had all my love, and I still had all my love left."

The boys watched the bright candles for a moment.

"What's that big red one for?" Jake asked.

"This candle is for Mark," Rhonda said, with a smile at her husband, who sat quietly across the room. "When I married Mark, I gave him all my love," she said, lighting the red candle with her blue one. "But Carl still has all my love. . . ."

"And so do I," Jake said with a grin.

"And I still have all my love left," Rhonda finished. Then she reached into her pocket and pulled out a tiny birthday candle.

"Guess what this candle is?" she asked her boys.

"The baby?" they answered.

"That's right. And when this baby is born, I'll give it all my love. Mark will have all my love, and Carl will have all my love, and Jake will have all my love, and I'll still have all my love left. That's how love is. See how much bright love we're going to have in this family?"

They sat together in silence, watching the flickering candles. Then Carl tugged at his mother's elbow. "Mom, can I light the baby's candle with my candle? I want to share my love."

Rhonda nodded and blew out the birthday candle, and Carl carefully picked up his candle and lit the tiny one. Jake took a turn lighting the baby candle himself, as did Mark.

Rhonda looked at her two boys and put her arm around Mark. "This will be our baby," she said, "and Mark and I will need your help to take care of him or her. Will you help us, guys?"

The next months passed quickly. The fighting didn't disappear, but both Carl and Jake enjoyed shopping for baby things, helping their mom and Mark fix up a room for the new baby, and thinking about names for boys and girls. They were thrilled when they got to hear the baby's heartbeat at the doctor's office. Carl provided the crowning touch when he placed the tiny birthday candle on the baby's new dresser.

"We're a family," he announced proudly, with a quick look at his stepfather. "And there's lots of love to go around."

Is it necessary to have a baby to unify your stepfamily? Of course not. Whatever sort of family you have—yours, mine, or ours—there are many ways to send the message of respect, belonging, and perhaps, even love to your children and stepchildren, and to understand the beliefs and longings behind their behavior.

6

The Ties That Bind

Understanding Loyalty
in Your Stepfamily

Q: My daughter wants to call her stepfather "Dad." Knowing this might upset her real father, she then suggested calling her birth father "Daddy" to make a notable difference but to give each special recognition in her life. Real dad isn't going for it. What acceptable terms of endearment are appropriate for a five-year-old to refer to her stepdad other than his first name?

A: What each parent is called is usually less important than the meaning behind the words. Many stepparents and birth parents wrestle over names and endearments, but the real issue is usually "Who is the 'real' parent? Who is most important?" Children always know the difference between their birth parents and stepparents. They are capable of loving and respecting many adults, but they hate having to choose among them.

Children look for belonging and significance—hence the desire to strengthen a relationship with stepdad by calling him "Dad." Adults want belonging and significance, too—hence birth dad's reluctance to allow his daughter to use that special term for her stepfather. There are many loving words for "father": you could try "Poppa" or "Pops," or check a foreign language dictionary for words that mean "dad" in other languages. Even a first name can be used when it is spoken with respect. Whatever your daughter calls the special men in her life, each will have a unique place in her heart.

The Name Game

WHY DOES IT seem to matter so much to so many adults what their children—and stepchildren—call them? In many families, the "name game" takes on powerful significance, as birth parents and stepparents vie for their children's respect and affection.

In truth, building loving relationships with the members of your family need not be a competition. Names are usually important because of what adults believe they signify: being special to a child, being recognized as the "real" parent, having a child's (or a partner's) respect and acceptance.

Names, especially "Mother" and "Father," are powerful symbols of loyalty and connection. William Doherty, Ph.D., a professor and director of the Marriage and Family Therapy Program at the University of Minnesota, has written that

> *Parental loyalty to children has been seen most often as a "covenantal" commitment as opposed to a "contractual" commitment. Rich in religious tradition, the idea of covenant conveys irrevocability: God will always love and do right by his own, no matter how they behave. Similarly, parents must always love and do right by their children, no matter how they behave. . . . Indeed, parental loyalty—the unbreakable, preferential commit-*

*ment to one's children—was so taken for granted that it is not even
included in the Ten Commandments. Perhaps abandoning one's child
was so unthinkable to the ancient Hebrews that no commandment was
necessary.* (*Family Therapy Networker,* May/June 1999, p. 35)

As a society, we expect parents to honor their obligation to their children.
We assume children should be able to grow up in families in which they are
nurtured, protected, loved, and taught, and we are horrified when parents
abuse or neglect their children. Because motherhood and fatherhood are
seen as a sacred commitment, many parents are
reluctant to make room for other "parents" in their
children's lives.

Remarriage creates a dilemma in most families.
Who is entitled to that special loyalty? Who gets to
say *my* son or *my* mom? Who comes first in my
heart? Most of us recognize eventually that names
are, after all, only words. No matter what the members of stepfamilies call each other, if those terms
are used with courtesy and affection everyone can
adjust. Loyalty issues are about belonging: who be-
longs to whom, and where, and how much? Understanding and accepting the
numerous and sometimes conflicting loyalties that are part of any stepfamily
is one of the most complicated issues you, your partner, and your children
must face.

> Understanding and
> accepting the
> numerous, sometimes
> conflicting loyalties in
> any stepfamily is one of
> the most complicated
> issues you must face.

What Does Loyalty Have to Do with Your Stepfamily?

TODD'S STEPFATHER IS a real grouch about the chores; he expects everything to be done immediately and is never satisfied with the results. "If your
dad had done his job," he grumbles, "I wouldn't have to fight with you over
this stuff." Todd, 15 and torn between wanting to please his stepfather and defend his dad, finally explodes one Saturday afternoon. "My dad did a good job.
You're not my dad," he shouts, "and I don't have to listen to you!"

At the house down the street, Jeremy, also 15, is sitting in the family room watching TV while his stepdad, Jim, talks on the phone. "I've been teaching my son to drive, and he's handling the stick shift pretty well," Jim says, "although he doesn't always look where he's going." Jeremy hears the phrase "my son" and smiles to himself; he likes his stepfather and is pleased to know his feelings are returned—so pleased, in fact, that he doesn't even say, "I do *too* look where I'm going!"

Loyalty—the notion of whom we give our allegiance and devotion to—is a powerful motivator in human behavior. Some of the most honored acts of human heroism and sacrifice have been inspired by loyalty to family, friends, God, and country. In stepfamilies, however, loyalties can feel muddy and complicated, clouded by the assumption so many parents and children make that they must "choose."

> In stepfamilies loyalties can feel muddy and complicated, clouded by the assumption so many parents and children make that they must "choose."

The difficulty occurs when enjoying closeness with one member means pulling away from another.

Amber is nine years old and spends time with both her mother alone and her father and stepmother. "When I come back from my dad's house," she says, "I always say I didn't have very much fun, even when I did. I don't want to hurt my mom's feelings. And when I'm at my dad's, I tell him I wish I could be with him more. Sometimes I feel bad that I'm saying stuff that isn't really true. But I don't want to make anybody feel hurt." Amber sighs.

It's easy enough to say that adults and children should be free to love and enjoy all the people in their lives, but when parents are honest, they often admit that letting go and creating space for that to happen feels very threatening.

Dealing with Children's Divided Loyalties

ADULTS USUALLY STRUGGLE to heal from old relationships and adjust to new ones; for children the process can be overwhelming. Children often harbor secret hopes that their biological parents will get back together, even though circumstances (and the adults in question) make it clear that reuniting

is unlikely if not impossible. Still, a child who dreams of having her "real" family back someday may find it hard to accept a stepparent.

Adults often create conflict for children when they are unable to handle their own emotions in an appropriate, effective way. Cody's father and stepmother argue a lot, sometimes about him. Cody is willing to accept his stepmother, but when she fights with his dad, Cody's loyalty to his father bubbles up and he leaps to defend his father. He also worries that if he doesn't behave right, his new family will break up—just like his old one. The pressure Cody feels to keep everyone happy and to sort out who should come first in his life keeps him constantly off balance and doesn't do much for his behavior.

Insecurity causes problems, too. Patsy and her boyfriend struggle to feed and clothe their four children; they both work hard, but even with child support there never seems to be enough money to go around. Patsy's ex-husband has a good job, however, and recently married a woman who helped start an Internet company. They have a large house with a pool and can afford to take Patsy's children on fabulous vacations. Patsy is glad her ex is doing well but worries that her children will eventually want to spend most of their time where life is easy and filled with luxury. Her insecurity leads her to cling to her children and to make them feel guilty about enjoying their time with their dad, which, in turn, makes them want to pull farther away.

> Adults usually struggle to heal from old relationships and adjust to new ones; for children the process can be overwhelming.

Children often struggle to cope with the pressures—spoken and unspoken—that they feel from adults. Jason likes his new stepfather; he's fun and easy to talk to. But Jason also knows that his dad dislikes his stepdad and is angry at his mom for marrying him. Jason feels stuck; he loves his dad and doesn't want to be disloyal to him. Does that mean he shouldn't like his stepfather?

Heather lives with her father and does not know her mother very well. Heather knows adults often whisper about her mom's "drinking problem" when they think Heather isn't listening. But Heather's mom is sweet and rather sad on the rare occasions they're able to be together, and Heather feels fiercely protective of her. Now Dad has remarried, and he tells Heather that she is to call her new stepmother "Mom." Heather likes her stepmother, but she already has a mom. What is she supposed to do?

Yolanda, on the other hand, was excited about her new stepfamily and wanted to call her stepmother "Mom." Her stepmother told Yolanda to please call her Evelyn.

Too often adults become set in their opinions about how things "should" be and forget to consider the feelings of their children and to be open to new possibilities. Adults could learn so much from children if they would take the time to "get into their world" and to consult with their children about ideas on how things could be done. This does not mean children should rule the roost; it does mean that involving children in a communication and problem-solving process is both helpful and respectful. Family meetings can be an effective way to encourage such communication and problem solving.

> Adults could learn so much from children if they would take the time to "get into their world" and to consult with their children about ideas on how things could be done.

Sometimes children are not consciously aware of what they feel but are encouraged and relieved when parents help them sort out their feelings. Getting into a child's world requires having some knowledge of a child's development and personality, and then making some guesses. Children will let you know whether you guess correctly. Guessing what a child may be thinking or feeling is effective only when you are ready to set aside your own prejudices and are truly curious.

Children are often open and willing to accept new relationships—unless they pick up other attitudes from their parents. One attitude that adults may try to foist off on children is divided loyalties.

It is generally easier for children to respect and love all of the adults in their lives than to be forced to choose among them. Children usually can learn to be comfortable with both a father and a stepfather, a mother and a stepmother, when they are allowed to take their time, encouraged to explore their feelings, and not forced to make either/or decisions.

> It is generally easier for children to respect and love all of the adults in their lives than to be forced to choose among them.

If you suspect that your child is struggling with divided loyalties, here are some suggestions to consider:

1. If the adults are creating conflict, stop it. Yes, it's difficult, but take a deep breath and relax a little. Unless you know that your child is being mistreated or neglected in his other parent's home, give him permission to build a relationship with all of the adults in his life. When he is with you, invite him to talk about his other family or parent. You need not be thrilled, but you can

COPING WITH DIVIDED LOYALTIES

1. If the adults are creating conflict, stop it.

2. If the child is creating conflict, understand it.

3. Remember that what you feel can be different from what you do.

4. Have faith in your relationship with your child.

listen calmly. Avoid going too far, though; don't pump a child for information for your own purposes.

If listening seems too difficult, consider getting help from a counselor, a pastor, or a friend. Forcing a child to choose sides rarely produces a healthy, happy family—for anyone. Learn to deal with your own emotions honestly; avoid dumping them on your child.

2. If the child is creating conflict, understand it. Create opportunities to listen and explore feelings, perhaps during your special time together. Let your child know that it's normal to have lots of feelings about a new family and that feelings are okay. Let her know, too, that you do not need her to choose sides.

> Forcing a child to choose sides rarely produces a healthy, happy family—for anyone.

Many parents struggle to decide how much they should tell children about their own feelings and decisions. It may help your child resolve her divided loyalties if she understands what is going on for you. She may need to be reminded that a reconciliation is not possible, that she need not choose between adults, or that she is not "required" to feel any particular emotion.

Remember that children's behavior is often motivated by their need to feel belonging and significance. Finding ways to help each child in your family belong will—eventually—enable them to stop creating division and accept reality.

3. Remember that what you feel can be different from what you do. It is a rare parent who doesn't feel a bit threatened and apprehensive when his or her child acquires a stepparent, especially if that stepparent is pretty cool! You will undoubtedly feel torn from time to time between the various members of your family, but that does not mean you need to *act* out of insecurity, jealousy, or anger. Acknowledge and take care of your own feelings, and do your best to treat your child, his other parent, his stepparent, and your stepchildren with respect.

4. Have faith in your relationship with your child. Despite the inevitable ups and downs of parenting, children usually know the difference between the adults in their lives and rarely want to replace one with another. An old saying states that if you truly want something to remain with you, you first must set it free. It may feel uncomfortable and seem paradoxical, but if you can offer your child faith, affection, and room to explore, the chances are good that your relationship will grow stronger than ever.

"The Kids Come First": What If Your Partner Leaves You Out?

WHEN RELATIONSHIPS ARE new, everyone has a tendency to be on his or her best behavior. You may make a real effort to get to know your partner's children, and you may be genuinely impressed by his or her devotion to parenting. When everyone is living together, however, the situation can get a bit more complicated.

Loyalty can be a problem not just between families but within them. Many stepparents come to the conclusion that they must compete for their partner's attention with that partner's children. And that can be a difficult task at best. After all, parents and their children form a tightly knit circle; they have been together all of the children's lives, and the circle often seems to exclude the new stepparent.

"My wife resists my efforts to get involved with her daughter," one stepdad reports. "I think she's afraid I'll do something wrong or hurt Abby's feelings. When Abby gets into trouble or has problems at school, she doesn't even tell me. I try not to take it personally, and I keep telling myself that it just takes time. But the truth is that it really hurts my feelings. I may not have a lot of experience being a father, but I'm willing to learn. And I wish my wife spent as much energy on her relationship with me as she does on Abby. Sometimes I wonder why she married me in the first place."

Parents and their birth children sometimes fail to recognize how difficult it can be to enter their charmed circle, share their history, and become a real part of their lives. And parents sometimes do believe that they must "protect" their children from a stepparent, particularly if that stepparent lacks experience, prefers his or her own children, assumes too much authority too soon, or says and does hurtful things.

> Loyalty can be a problem not just between families but within them.

If you are feeling left out of the family circle (or suspect that you've excluded your partner), find a relaxed moment and share your feelings with your partner, perhaps at one of your couple's meetings. The instinct to protect one's children does sometimes lead parents to behave in ways that are damaging to the other relationships in the family. Ask for your partner's help, and respectfully look together for solutions. Feelings that are left unexpressed and unresolved sometimes go underground; the resentment that builds up can damage your family and your future together.

Dealing with Parents' Divided Loyalties

LOYALTY ISSUES AFFECT everyone in a stepfamily in some way. Why do the members of stepfamilies so often believe they have to choose among the people in their lives, instead of being able to love all of them? Children aren't the only ones who struggle with divided loyalties; obviously, adults also wrestle with the pressure to decide who should come first.

We have discussed the importance of putting your relationship with your spouse first. Parents who put their relationship first are able to present a united front. This united front is not "against" the children but is a stand for cooperation "with" the children. When children are allowed to come first, not only is the couple divided, but also the children usually become manipulative. Of course, most children practice the fine art of manipulation even when their biological parents are together (e.g., trying to get one parent to say yes after the other has said no), but they find fuel for the fire when their biological parent takes their side against a stepparent. Even though attempts at manipulation are normal, allowing children to get away with it is unhealthy—stepfamily or not!

Putting their relationship first does not mean that parents should be neglectful of children. In fact, children should be such a close second that the difference is hardly noticeable. It is never okay to treat children with disrespect or to ignore their needs and feelings. Putting their relationship first means that parents collaborate as they learn to perform the juggling and balancing acts of their family circus. It also helps children feel more secure and gives them a good model for their own successful relationships.

Stepfamily life sometimes seems like a never-ending series of choices. What are your priorities? Why does it so often seem like there's not enough of you to go around? What happens when adults focus on their own relationships at the expense of their children?

"My mom left me when she met Randy," said 17-year-old Amanda. "She said she'd been alone for too long, and she wanted to have a life of her own. I guess she was tired of being a mom and thought I was old enough to take care of myself. Anyway, Randy is ten years younger than she is, and he didn't want a teenager around. Now I'm living with my dad and his wife; they have little kids, and I feel like I'm competing for their attention. Sometimes it feels like no one wants me."

"I'm tired of being the baby-sitter," complained 14-year-old Sam. "Ever since my dad married Lauren, they've spent all their free time together. They expect me to watch Lauren's little boy, and I never have time for myself. Now Lauren is saying my dad should send me away to military school. I feel like my dad loves Lauren a lot more than he loves me. I've been thinking about going to live with my mom in Oklahoma, but I don't want to leave my friends. I don't know what to do."

> Feelings that are left unexpressed and unresolved sometimes go underground; the resentment that builds can damage your family and your future together.

It's not difficult to understand the pain these young people feel, yet if you asked their parents what they felt, you might get a different picture of what is going on. Is it wrong to enjoy being with someone you love and to want time with him or her?

It is true that the couple's relationship forms the foundation for a healthy family and that investing time and energy in the relationship is wise. Yet here, as in so many other areas in stepfamily life, balance is the ideal. The couple's relationship comes first *as long as* the children are being treated respectfully and their needs are being met. Neglecting the children to concentrate on your partner is not in the best interests of your children—or your family.

> It is never okay to treat children with disrespect or to ignore their needs and feelings.

Like it or not, building a relationship with someone who has children is a package deal: You can't have one without the other. As we have learned, parents have an obligation to nurture and care for their children. Many stepparents are waiting eagerly for the day their stepchildren leave home, but consider for a moment: If you force your partner to choose between you and his children or actively try to maneuver even a difficult child out of the home, you are creating a situation that may ultimately destroy your relationship—and damage that child for life. It can be extremely challenging to be a stepparent, particularly when your stepchild resists you or behaves in troubling ways, but rejecting or neglecting the child is not an option.

Learning to accept and resolve the situation will take time, patience, and ingenuity. Get the children involved in the balancing and juggling acts. Ask for their help in finding solutions that meet the needs of everyone. Kids are great at finding solutions when they are invited to do so and are taught the skills for brainstorming (which we will discuss later, in the family meeting chapter). As long as you focus on solutions, you can avoid complaining and blaming.

Practicing the skills we've already suggested will help you be sure that everyone's feelings and needs are being heard. Special time with your children will help you and your partner stay in touch with them; family meetings will give everyone a chance to air grievances, avoid taking sides, and look for solutions. Good listening and communication skills allow everyone to express thoughts and feelings, and to feel heard—adults included.

Coping with Guilt

DON HAS A problem. He has one son, who lives with his mother, and he recently married Kathleen, a wonderful, affectionate wife, and also the mother of two boys, who live with them. Don found that he was often angry with his stepsons; he found fault with them for small things, ignored their attempts to spend time with him, and was never happy with their grades. The boys felt angry and hurt; the bickering and fighting upset Kathleen. Finally, Kathleen suggested that they go to counseling to figure out what to do. It was in the therapist's office that the truth hit Don.

"I miss my own son," he told Kathleen. "I feel like a bad father because I'm not with him as much as I used to be and because I left his mom. Now I'm spending my days with two boys who aren't mine, and I feel guilty. I guess I thought that rejecting your sons meant I was staying loyal to my own. But all I've done is make a mess and make everyone unhappy. I'm really sorry, hon," Don said quietly.

Don's feelings aren't difficult to understand. The loyalties and connections in stepfamilies can pull even the most caring adults in several directions. Stepfathers in particular tend to struggle with their feelings about which children should be most important: physical custody often goes to mothers, which means fathers are most likely to be the parent who sees children only on weekends and holidays. When fathers remarry, they often find themselves living with their new wife's children and missing their own. Guilt may follow—and guilt rarely brings out the best in people.

> The couple's relationship comes first *as long as* the children are being treated respectfully and their needs are being met.

Most stepparents wonder whether they will ever love their stepchildren as much, or in the same way, as they love their own. And the answer is "Maybe not." But as we've suggested before, "more" or "the same" need not be an issue. When each child in a family feels a sense of belonging and significance and is treated with respect and dignity, everyone can feel comfortable. Do avoid overt favoritism; children notice who gets the most presents at holidays, the biggest room, and the best

Discouraged children misbehave; if any of the children in your stepfamily feel overlooked or unwanted, you are likely to be the target of behavior you don't enjoy.

special activities, and those tangible things become symbols for love and belonging. Discouraged children misbehave; if any of the children in your stepfamily feel overlooked or unwanted, you are likely to be the target of behavior you don't enjoy.

Don discovered that drawing his stepsons into the circle of his affection was easier than he had thought. He began looking for what the boys did well, encouraging them, and spending time doing things they enjoyed. As he got to know them better, he recognized that his relationships with them would never be the same as that he shared with his own son—but that they could still enjoy being together. His guilt ebbed away as he discovered that he could build strong ties with all three of the boys. When his own son came to visit, Don spent time alone with him but also invited all of the boys to hang out with him. As time passed, they learned to accept each other, with only the usual amount of bickering and hassle!

Loyalty is a subtle but strong influence on the way members of stepfamilies connect—or fail to connect—with each other. If you spend some time thinking it over, you will undoubtedly discover many ways you, your partner, and the children you share have been tugged and pulled by old and new relationships. If you can find the courage to help everyone give up the need to choose, you may find that stepfamily life becomes far more harmonious.

7

Back and Forth

Dealing with Your Child's Other Parent

By this time you may be thinking, "This stepfamily stuff is pretty complex. There's so much to consider." But, as the commercial says, "Wait—there's more!" The reality for most stepfamilies is that somewhere out there are the children's other parents, which, in turn, may mean all sorts of complicated problems and feelings.

We recognize that not everyone in a stepfamily has experienced a divorce, so we must ask for the patience of those who believe this information does not apply to them. Still, the vast majority of adults who are blending their families have been through at least one divorce, with far-reaching effects on them and on their children. If *both* adults in the new family have ex-partners to contend with, stepfamily life can feel unbelievably complicated. After all, these are people who couldn't get along as partners. How on earth are they supposed to deal with each other now?

Dozens of issues emerge. What if you and your ex can't even talk to each other? What if your ex's new partner is making all the decisions? How do you fit the vacation and activity schedules of two or three families together and keep your dignity and sanity? What if your child's other parent never calls or visits? What if he or she doesn't contribute to your child's support? What if you don't like the way your child is treated at her other home?

In her excellent book, *Mom's House, Dad's House: Making Two Homes for Your Child* (Fireside/Simon & Schuster, 1980, revised 1997), Isolina Ricci

suggests dealing with divorce and remarriage as the *reorganization* of a family, not its destruction. The goal, she says, is to create "two homes with no fighting." Most adults understand that children tend to do best when they are able to have open, healthy relationships with both parents and when all adults involved are able to build amicable, respectful relationships. Most are aware that open hostility, negative and critical remarks about the other parent (even when they're true), and manipulative actions and comments can be devastating to children, creating both conflict and the divided loyalties we've already discussed.

> The sheer logistical complexity of communicating, synchronizing schedules, and working out the inevitable differences of opinion can be overwhelming.

Yet sometimes the temptation to strike back is strong. Having to deal week after week with someone you've already decided you don't want to live with (or with someone who has rejected you) can be highly frustrating. It is easy to forget how much the fighting, arguing, and revenge hurts children, especially when your own feelings and needs seem more important. Even when parents truly desire to get along and "coparent" their children peacefully and effectively, the sheer logistical complexity of communicating, synchronizing schedules, and working out the inevitable differences of opinion can be overwhelming.

Like it or not, when you share a child with someone, that person remains a part of your life for years. You may have heard stories about couples who are very comfortable as divorced coparents. Both attend their children's sports functions and other special events; sometimes they even have pizza together afterward. One ex-husband even gave his ex-wife and her new husband his king-sized bed and slept on the couch when they came to visit the children. Other parents can barely tolerate their ex-spouses.

Is it truly possible for ex-partners to share their children's lives, for new mates to feel included, and for children to move calmly between homes with different rules and lifestyles? Not always, perhaps, since we are human and often make mistakes. But it is certainly possible to build a working partnership where all adults involved cooperate respectfully to raise children. Children, as well as adults, are invariably better off for it.

Back and Forth: Building a Working Partnership

EVEN PARENTS WHO couldn't get along as marriage partners can work together as parents. Building a working coparenting relationship, however, means breaking old patterns of relating to one another and learning new ones. It means learning to communicate with your child's stepparent, to make room in the decision-making process for another set of opinions and ideas. It means sharing an interest in children's activities and feelings and sharing responsibility for their care. It means working out financial and visitation arrangements. It means understanding that your children suffer when they want to love and be loved by both of their parents and, instead, get caught in the middle. It also means accepting the difficult truth that you probably can't change your ex-partner, his or her new partner, or the way he or she chooses to run a household. You can, however, work toward cooperation and understanding.

> Like it or not, when you share a child with someone, that person remains a part of your life for years.

Richard knocked on the door to his daughter's room. Danielle, 17, was lying on the bed with headphones on, listening to music and thumbing idly through a magazine. She was also smoking a cigarette.

"Hey," Richard said, pulling at the headphones. "What do you think you're doing? You know we don't smoke. Your room stinks to high heaven, and you're probably going to set it on fire one of these days. Look at me when I'm talking to you, young lady!"

Danielle let her gaze linger on the page for a moment, then looked coolly up at her father. "What are you so uptight about? Everybody smokes."

"You mean your mother smokes," Richard said. "Just because she does it doesn't mean that you can. At least, not in my house."

Danielle shook her head. "Mom is a lot easier to get along with than you are. You and Carol are so strict; you don't let me do anything. Smoking is cool. Anyway, you can't stop me—I'll just do it when you're not around. I'm going over to Marie's house."

Danielle made her exit, and Richard drew in a deep breath—and coughed. Just then Carol, his new wife, walked in. "Phew," she said, wrinkling her nose. "What's going on in here?"

"Danielle's been smoking—again. I don't know what I'm going to do with her. She knows it's bad for her health and that I don't like it, but her friends all do it. Worst of all, her mom smokes and doesn't seem to mind if Danielle does. She's so irresponsible!"

Carol reached up and massaged the back of Richard's neck. "Linda does things differently, that's for sure, but she seems to be a pretty good mom most of the time. Maybe you should give her a call."

"I can't talk to Linda, Carol. You know that."

"Well, you've certainly had your problems in the past. But isn't Danielle's health worth giving it another try?" Carol asked.

Richard drove Danielle back to her mother's house the next day and, instead of dropping her off at the curb, walked with his daughter to the front door.

"Where are you going, Dad?" Danielle asked.

"I want to talk to your mom for a moment," Richard replied.

Danielle looked startled, then raised her eyebrows. "This ought to be good," she said as she opened the door and walked down the hall to her room.

> Even parents who couldn't get along as marriage partners can work together as parents.

Richard paused on the threshold and called out his ex-wife's name. When Linda appeared, he held up his hand before she could say anything.

"I know the last time I came by we wound up yelling," Richard said, "but I want to try again. I'm worried about Danielle."

"What is it?" Linda asked, a bit suspiciously.

"She's been smoking in our house. I know you smoke, and I also know we probably can't keep her from doing it if she's determined to. But I wanted to talk to you and see what ideas you might have."

"Come in, Richard," Linda said and sat down on the sofa. "It seems like all Danielle's friends smoke these days. And I haven't been a real terrific example for her, I'm afraid. But I'm thinking about quitting."

Richard threw his hands up in the air. "You've said that for years. And you never follow through. You always. . . ." Richard caught himself and gave Linda a rueful grin. "Bad habits," he said, sitting down in a chair. "Can I start over?"

Linda nodded, looking more interested as Richard continued. "I know we haven't always agreed on things, including about Danielle. But I know you love her as much as I do. I want her to be healthy and to know that both of her parents will do everything they can to help her. Carol and I want to work with you on this. We're going to ask Danielle not to smoke in the house; if she wants to smoke at our place, she'll have to go outside. We just wanted you to know that."

> Focusing on the matter at hand, using effective communication skills, and working patiently toward mutual understanding can help defuse potentially explosive situations.

Linda sat quietly for a moment, thinking. Then she said, "Maybe it's time I got healthy myself. Maybe I really should quit."

Suddenly Richard and Linda became aware that Danielle was standing in the doorway, watching and listening. "You guys have never agreed on anything," she said. "What's going on?"

Linda looked at Richard, then at her daughter. "We may fight sometimes, but we do care about you—both of us. And maybe we can cooperate better than we have in the past. Danielle, I guess we can't stop you from smoking, but

I'm going to try to quit and I hope you will, too. Regardless, from now on all smoking here and at your dad's will have to happen outside. Okay?"

Danielle looked at her mom and dad, then rolled her eyes. "Whatever," she said. But there was a trace of a smile on her face as she walked back to her room.

Coparenting in Action

EX-PARTNERS WON'T agree on everything, and old disagreements may get dragged into current issues. Still, you don't have to love the people at your workplace to be able to work together respectfully; coparenting can be the same. Focusing on the matter at hand instead of on old emotional issues, using effective communication skills, and working patiently toward mutual understanding can help defuse potentially explosive situations.

> Each ex-partner should consider drawing up a "parenting plan," a document that outlines rights and responsibilities on important issues.

Because so many children go back and forth between homes, it is immensely helpful to have a clear and consistent arrangement for how issues, schedules, responsibilities, and financial arrangements will be handled. Each set of ex-partners should consider drawing up a "parenting plan," a document that outlines rights and responsibilities on important issues. Many divorcing parents have such a plan as part of their divorce documents, but remarriages often change the landscape a bit, and it is usually wise to take another look.

The legal issues of support and visitation are beyond the scope of this book, but in general terms, the law usually acknowledges that children do best when they have open, reasonable contact with both parents. If you are unable to deal calmly with your child's other parent, you might consider getting help from a professional mediator or therapist who specializes in these issues. (Your local family law court may be able to give you some referrals.) The Parenting Plan box (page 100) outlines some issues to consider in drawing up a parenting plan.

What If Your Ex Just Won't Cooperate?

Q: I have been married for six months. My wife and her ex have tolerated each other for the kids' sake, and I respected this. We even got together to do family things. The kids and I get along very well, and I love them and their mom dearly. The problem is that just recently the kids told us their daddy has been drinking a lot and driving with them in the car and that he and his friends smoke pot. My wife blew up and confronted him, and he admitted he did these things but says it's not a big problem. So my wife decided not to let him have the children any more.

We want the kids' dad to be a part of their lives, but we can't risk losing them in a drunk driving accident or having them around people who are doing things that are illegal. Now he and his friends are calling here and threatening us, and the kids are upset. We don't know what to do. How do we explain this to our children?

A: Many stepdads (and stepmoms) find that the issue that most threatens their new family is dealing with the ex. It would be worthwhile to check with your local district attorney or legal aid office to see exactly what the laws in your community provide with respect to custody and visitation. Your stepchildren's father has certain legal rights (unless he does something serious enough to have them terminated). It may be a good idea to report the problem to Children's Protective Services, which will keep the call confidential. Their father is endangering the children by drinking, drugging, and driving with them.

Your first priority must be the safety of your stepchildren, but if your wife and her ex have joint legal custody, you may not be able to bar him from seeing the children. Remain respectful; getting hooked into trading insults (or even blows) will not help. It's also important to tell your children the truth in simple, respectful terms. You don't need to bash their father to do this. You can simply tell them that you want them to see and love their dad but you also need to keep them safe, and their father is making

> It is wise to realize that you cannot change your child's other parent.

> # YOUR PARENTING PLAN:
> ## ISSUES TO CONSIDER
>
> Life in your stepfamily will go much more smoothly when you and the other adults in your child's life can agree on these issues:
>
> - Visitation schedules (overnights, midweek visits, summers, holidays, and special events)
>
> - Custody: legal and/or physical
>
> - Responsibility: Who will make which decisions? Do stepparents have a right to participate?
>
> - Education, college, and expenses
>
> - Medical and dental care and insurance
>
> - Mental health care
>
> - Other insurance: life insurance or car insurance (for teenagers)
>
> - Child care (be sure to include pickup and drop-off instructions that are specific about stepparents' rights)
>
> - Religious training

some poor choices right now. You may arrange for them to talk to him regularly on the phone, exchange e-mail or other messages, or have supervised visits with him in a neutral place. You and your wife can work together to give the children space to love—and learn about—their birth father on their own.

Unfortunately, not all parents are willing or able to maintain a loving, respectful relationship with their children. Some disappear completely; others

- Parenting education

- Contact with extended family (visits with grandparents and other family members)

- Moving: Can either family move out of town and take the children?

- Activities (sports, music, clubs, etc.): Who will pay? Drive? Attend?

- Transportation

- Access to school and other records

- Tax consequences: Who gets the deduction for each child?

- How will changes in schedules be handled?

- How will disagreements be resolved?

If your children are old enough, be sure to invite their ideas and solutions as you discuss these issues. Teenagers in particular deserve to have some say about how schedules should be arranged.

refuse to contribute time or resources or are maddeningly inconsistent about showing up, keeping agreements, or spending time with children. It is wise to realize that you cannot change your child's other parent. You can offer suggestions, attend parenting classes together, or even provide a copy of this book, but you are likely to accomplish far more by working with your children to understand that their other parent's behavior is not their fault and teaching them ways to cope.

Settling Down: Creating Two Healthy Families for Your Children

COPARENTING ISN'T NECESSARY; children can grow up happy and healthy with just one loving, committed parent. But building a respectful working relationship with your ex-partner (and your new partner's ex) can benefit all of you and make stepfamily life much easier. The Building a Coparenting Relationship box provides some ideas to consider.

1. Take children out of the middle. Don't encourage divided loyalties; that is, don't ask children to carry messages, spy on their other parent, or choose sides. Make every effort to communicate directly with your ex-partner. If that is impossible, consider seeing a counselor or using a mediator to work out disagreements. Don't use your child's relationship with his other parent or the time they spend together as a punishment or reward for behavior. Recognize that your child wants to spend time with both of you.

2. Offer respect and dignity. Remember the old Golden Rule? You may not respect your ex (or your new partner's ex), but remember that there can be a difference between what you feel and what you do. Tough as it may be, try to treat your child's other parent (and stepparent) as you would like to be treated. Don't blame your ex for every problem or criticize his or her habits, personality, or choices to your children. Even when it seems that you do not receive equal consideration in return, do your best to communicate respectfully. Corny as it sounds, what you send out often returns to you. Your children will

BUILDING A COPARENTING RELATIONSHIP

1. Take children out of the middle.

2. Offer respect and dignity.

3. Create structure and keep agreements.

4. Decide where stepparents fit in.

5. Work together to ease transitions.

6. Share information.

7. Don't be a "Disneyland parent."

benefit from your attitude of mutual respect—even if your ex-partner never shares it.

3. Create structure and keep agreements. Creating a parenting plan will help everyone in your stepfamily know what to expect, which can help you avoid a great deal of confusion and conflict. Whether or not you have a written document in hand, be aware that consistency and predictability help everyone work together smoothly.

Most families find it much easier to handle the back-and-forth of shared custody when there is a schedule firmly in place. Although unexpected changes of plan are inevitable, do your best to keep the agreements you make. When you cannot, let your child's other parent know in advance, and work together to make new arrangements.

4. Decide where stepparents fit in. Some families prefer that a child's biological parents make decisions together regarding activities, visitation, and schedules; others involve stepparents in all decisions affecting family life. In fact, if talking calmly with your ex-partner is just too difficult, you may find it easier to make plans and discuss problems with your child's stepparent. How you do things is less important than whether what you do is respectful and effective.

Keep the lines of communication open; in fact, it may help to have all the significant adults in a child's life meet occasionally to solve problems and discuss needs and wishes. You may want to attend a parenting class together. Remember, you can't force your child's other parent to change; you can work to create a loving, respectful, trusting atmosphere in your own home.

> Don't use your child's relationship with his other parent or the time they spend together as a punishment or reward for behavior.

5. Work together to ease transitions. Many parents remark that their children's behavior changes each time they return from their other parent's home. Going back and forth can be difficult for children, especially when their parents' lifestyles and rules are very different. Children often find it necessary to test their boundaries each time they change homes; remaining kind and firm at the same time (more on that later) about the rules in your own home will help.

Use routine charts to help children track their possessions, clothing (few things are more upsetting on a busy morning than realizing that all your child's clothes are at the *other* parent's house), and school materials. With practice and patience, children learn to be responsible about keeping track of what belongs where. Having some personal space and storage at each home will help, too.

Make time for listening to your children. If you have justified concerns about their health or safety at their other parent's home, express your worries to your ex-partner and, if necessary, to the proper authorities. Sometimes, because of physical or sexual abuse or other serious problems, it may not be in your child's best interest to spend time with his or her other parent. Remember, though, that children usually continue to love a parent even when they understand that the parent's behavior and choices are not wise.

6. Share information. Information about your child's activities, health, and academic progress can be a valuable tool to help families stay connected—

or it can become a powerful weapon in the war for a child's affection. The Golden Rule works here, too. Try to let your child's other parent know the things you would want to know in his or her place. Remember, your child will benefit from having two families with no conflict. Inform your ex-partner about school conferences, soccer games, and illnesses. If you cannot talk calmly, try using e-mail or voice mail to share important information.

7. Don't be a "Disneyland parent." Trying to win children over or strengthen your relationship with them by providing treats and privileges, trips, or other special things can be extremely tempting. When parents truly care for their children, however, they recognize that presents are not the way to build a healthy relationship and that children are not prizes in a bidding war. Remember your long-range goals for your children and stepfamily? Think about the decisions that children might be making. Will they decide that love is something that can be purchased? Over time, trust, respect, security, encouragement, and love mean more to children than presents and privileges; the best memories often are made at home for little or no money.

> Try to let your child's other parent know the things you would want to know in his or her place.

If your child's other parent has fallen victim to the Disneyland parent syndrome, avoid being baited into argument or jealousy. Trust yourself, deal honestly with your emotions and fears, and focus on your goals for your own family.

When Children "Work the System"

SOONER OR LATER, it happens in almost every stepfamily. The day comes when a child looks his parent right in the eye and says, "I don't want to live with you anymore. I want to go live with Mom [or Dad]." It is a rare parent who can hear that particular threat without feeling a confusing mixture of anger, hurt, and alarm.

Children may make such a devastating statement for any number of reasons. The threat almost always gets them attention, and it can create a pleasing feeling of power, especially when adults react strongly. Sometimes children feel wounded and want to hurt others as they feel hurt; sometimes they are so discouraged that anything (or anywhere) else seems preferable. Children learn to play one parent against another even when those parents are married, but the ploy becomes even more effective when parents no longer live together. Or the need may be real—a child may have compelling reasons for wanting to live with his other parent.

Learning about the mistaken goals of behavior (chapter 12) will help you understand what's behind your child's words. She may simply need to spend more time with her other parent. In fact, listening calmly and saying (without anger or sarcasm), "Well, that may be something we should talk about," may take much of the magic out of the threat.

How should you respond if your child truly wants to live with her other parent? This is easier said than done: Try not to overreact. Use active listening and emotional honesty (see the next chapter) to talk through the problem; usually this approach is enough to resolve it peacefully. Do try to consider the wishes of your children and listen carefully for needs and feelings hidden in their words. Some parents aren't comfortable letting children decide where they will live, while others are able to involve children in the decision.

One mother said to her son, "You can go live with your dad, and you can change your mind and come back—once. I can understand your need to spend time with your dad; however, it's not okay to go back and forth every time you get mad at one of us or to move to avoid solving problems." This mom respected her son's needs but would not allow manipulation.

Listen to your heart, and trust your knowledge of your own children. Work toward balancing firmness with kindness; this is the best way to avoid manipulation and hurt feelings.

Your Attitude Is the Key

IF YOUR CHILD is lucky enough to have the love and active involvement of her other parent, that person (and, perhaps, his or her new partner) will be a part of your life as long as you share your child. Raising children means a lifetime of softball games, ballet recitals, school programs and conferences, graduations, weddings—all the events and celebrations that add much to life's meaning—and your child will probably want to see all of the adults she loves at these special times.

For better or worse, adults set the pace—and the tone—of these complicated relationships. If your attitude toward your ex-partner is one of mistrust and hostility, your child will react accordingly. If, however, you try to remain open, respectful, and cooperative, your child will follow your lead. Investing the time and energy to make your relationship with your child's other parent (and stepparent) a positive and healthy one may not be easy, but such an investment will spare everyone a great deal of pain and may lay the foundation for a healthier, happier life for you, your children, and your new family.

8

Breaking Down the Walls

Feelings and the Art of Communication

WE VE SPENT A fair amount of time looking at all the ways life in a stepfamily can be complicated and unsettling. But stepfamilies can be wonderful, too. Over and over again as we've explored the issues stepfamilies face, we've mentioned feelings. Everyone knows what feelings are, but what good are they? Don't feelings just create problems? Actually, feelings provide information about what is happening to you, what it means, and what you might need to do to make things better. Recognizing and dealing with emotions in healthy ways is a valuable tool you can use to help everyone in your family get along.

Feelings certainly *can* be overwhelming. Think for a moment about a time when you felt angry or depressed or lonely. What did you do with those feelings? How did you express them to the people around you?

Children, too, have strong feelings. In fact, their emotions are just as powerful as those of the adults around them, yet they often have even fewer effective skills for dealing with their emotions. Children learn about feelings—what they are and what to do with them—from their parents and the other significant adults in their lives. Unfortunately, all too often what they learn doesn't help them much.

> Recognizing and dealing with emotions in healthy ways is a valuable tool you can use to help everyone in your family get along.

What Exactly Is a Feeling?

FEELINGS ARE STANDARD equipment for human beings. In fact, your feelings are your barometer; they keep you tuned in to what is going on inside you, provide useful information (think, for example, of what you might attempt if you didn't have the emotion called "fear"), and help you know when you need to make changes in your life.

Feelings are neither good nor bad; everyone has them, and emotions by themselves don't cause problems. Even irrational feelings are not bad. (After all, who gets to decide that they are irrational?) However, what you do with your feelings can create difficulties for you and for those around you. Too many people blame their irrational acts on their feelings. Using your feelings for information and personal growth is much different from using them to justify destructive acts.

Chances are good that each member of your stepfamily has feelings—lots of them. How can you open the lines of communication among parents, stepparents, and children? Can you and your family learn to talk calmly and honestly about your feelings instead of acting them out?

Feelings have gotten a bad reputation because the ways people have learned to deal with them often do not work well. Most adults deal with difficult feelings either through emotional displays—dumping their emotions on the people around them—or by trying to squelch them entirely. The feelings you refuse to express do not go away, however; they simply go into hiding. Their energy remains, and those feelings will either leak out or explode when you least expect it. The results often are far more damaging than if the feelings had been expressed in the first place. Mature, healthy people have learned to express feelings with dignity and respect for themselves and others.

> It isn't always necessary to do something with your feelings; sometimes just letting yourself feel them is enough.

Many adults struggle with acknowledging and expressing their feelings. It often seems easier (or more "polite") to stifle what you feel. This mistaken pattern of denying feelings may be passed on to your children. For instance, an angry child may say, "I hate her—she's not my real mother!" An adult answers,

"Of course you don't hate her. We're a family now." But the truth is that at that particular moment, what the child feels is very real. It would be healthier to say, "I can see how angry you are right now. Let's talk about what happened." (Remember, the worst time to teach or negotiate is when negative feelings are high on either side.)

It isn't always necessary to *do* something with feelings; sometimes just letting yourself feel them (and learn from them) is enough. For instance, feeling guilty may be a cue to spend more time or energy on an important relationship; feeling anxious may be a signal to make a decision or face a troubling issue. The feelings often dissipate once you have understood their message. But because adults and children sometimes act on feelings without stopping to think about what they mean (and since living in a stepfamily can stir up so many feelings), learning to accept and express emotions without causing harm to yourself and those around you is important. How do you begin?

The Silent Message: Nonverbal Communication

COMMUNICATION COMES IN many forms. Adults are usually most comfortable with words; they use lots and lots of them (and then wonder why children tune them out). But sometimes the strongest messages you receive aren't expressed in words at all—they are sent nonverbally. In fact, some experts estimate that as much as 80 percent of what you "hear" from those around you is nonverbal.

Energy has a loud nonverbal voice, and your feelings create distinct energy. Energy does not lie, but people sometimes do. For example, you may feel upset. Your spouse can "feel" this in your energy and asks, "What's wrong?" Because you have not learned that feeling what you feel and expressing it with dignity and respect are okay, you say, "Nothing!" However, your nonverbal communication speaks louder than your words. Communication breaks down because your spouse "knows" something is wrong but is rebuked

> Some experts estimate that as much as 80 percent of what you "hear" from those around you is nonverbal.

for correctly reading your energy. This can be "crazy making," especially for children, who trust parents (even when they are wrong) more than their own feelings (even when they are accurate).

What is nonverbal communication, and why is it important? Nonverbal communication is a "voice" for the message of energy. You will be a better communicator when you understand this and learn to trust the feeling you get when reading the energy of nonverbal communication. Most adults place a great deal of meaning on the words that they hear, but words are frequently less accurate than the nonverbal clues being sent at the same time. It is interesting to note that children easily read the nonverbal communication of the adults around them; in fact, it is one of the most important ways they learn about their world during their early years—and one of their primary means of communicating feelings themselves.

For instance, a child's body language may express many feelings for which he doesn't yet have words. Infants first learn about feelings, trust, and belonging by reading the nonverbal messages sent by their parents: a warm tone of voice, a smiling face, a gentle touch all communicate the vital message "You are loved; you belong." Most parents have had the unsettling experience of being tense or nervous when they pick up a baby and having the baby stiffen and begin to cry.

Young children also are especially sensitive to the nonverbal messages adults send them. They can "read" energy long before they can speak or read words. And when an adult's words and nonverbal messages don't match, children instinctively trust the nonverbal part. For instance, Kathy is helping her stepfather prepare breakfast on a busy Monday morning. Kathy is doing her best, but she is only six, and the milk carton is too heavy for her small hands. When it slips from her grasp, she gasps in alarm and shoots a worried glance at her stepfather.

"Oh, I'm sorry," she says. "Are you mad?"

Kathy's stepfather is not having a good morning. He's late and has an important report due at the office, and he's been thinking that Kathy's mother should be fixing breakfast instead of him. Now he has a mess to clean up.

"No," he manages to say between clenched teeth. "It was an accident. Just get a sponge, Kathy."

"If you're not mad," Kathy offers timidly, "why are your eyebrows all scrunched up?"

Pay careful attention the next time you have a conversation with someone you love. Do you make eye contact with that person? Do they look back at you? What does your facial expression say? Your tone of voice? What about posture and body position? Do your nonverbal messages match the words you are saying? How does the other person respond, verbally and nonverbally?

If you're still wondering why this is important, consider this: Most of us say "I love you" almost carelessly, assuming that the words themselves are enough. But the next time you want a child you care about to really hear this message, get down on her level and establish eye contact. Use a warm tone of voice; smile at her. You may even want to place a gentle hand on her shoulder. Now tell her you love her. Can you feel a hug coming?

Sometimes our nonverbal messages make words unnecessary. Kevin is stretched out on the couch, an ice pack on his left knee. He worked hard all during his Little League season to make the All-Star team and he succeeded; unfortunately, he also injured his knee and is unable to play in the big tournament. Kevin is disappointed and angry, and well-intended words seem to make him even more prickly and miserable. But when his father walks by, he gives Kevin a sympathetic smile and squeezes his shoulder, and Kevin responds with a grateful look.

Children, too, constantly send nonverbal messages. Their facial expressions, gestures, and behavior provide clues about what they are feeling, and adults can use these clues to establish trust, understanding, and genuine communication.

In chapter 12 we will learn how to trust feelings to help us understand the mistaken goals behind behavior. It is important to teach children to understand and trust their feelings. One way to do this is through active listening.

The Art of Active Listening

THROUGHOUT THIS BOOK, we've offered stories—stories of parents, stepparents, and children trying to live together and to do the best they can. Woven through their stories (and through your own) are feelings. It is a wise person who can accept that human behavior generally grows from what we think, feel, and decide about ourselves. Learning to recognize feelings, express them in healthy ways, and accept the feelings of others are vital skills that may help you and those you love prevent the mistakes, arguments, and wrong choices that complicate your lives together.

> It is a wise person who accepts that human behavior generally grows from what we think, feel, and decide about ourselves.

Human beings have lots of different feelings; in fact, feelings sometimes change from moment to moment! But a number of emotions are especially familiar to members of stepfamilies. Most adults (and most children) must deal with feelings of grief and loss. They usually experience jealousy, insecurity, or anger at times. Behavior—both children's and adults'—is often a plea to have those feelings recognized and understood.

Ben was on his way to the garage when he heard loud crashes and angry muttering coming from the study. He poked his head in the door and found himself face to face with his 11-year-old stepson, Brian. And Brian obviously was not happy.

"What's up, Bud?" Ben asked. "It sounded like something fell in here. Are you okay?"

Brian glanced behind him, where a stack of books and papers lay scattered on the floor next to the desk. "I guess I knocked some stuff off," he said sullenly, and when he looked up at his stepfather, the spark of battle was in his eyes.

Ben sighed. Brian stayed with him and Jody, his wife, every other weekend; Ben's own 9-year-old daughter, Amy, lived with them full-time. Both children were fascinated by the computer and spent many hours playing games, and the computer had become a source of tension and conflict. Now, as Ben took a deep breath and faced his stepson, he could see how angry he was. He chose not to mention the books and papers thrown to the floor (that must have been the crash he'd heard) and resisted the urge to call for Jody. Instead, he concentrated on Brian. What had they suggested in that parenting class about moments like this?

Oh, yes, he thought—feelings. Perhaps that was a good place to start.

"You look pretty mad, Brian," Ben said as calmly as he could.

Brian didn't hesitate. "Amy wrecked my game," he said. "That's the second time she's wiped it out. It took me four days to get to level 7, and now I have to start all over!"

Ben kept himself from rushing to defend his daughter and continued to focus on Brian's feelings. "That must be pretty discouraging," he said. "No wonder you're upset."

Brian sensed his stepfather's newfound willingness to listen, and months of pent-up frustration began to pour out. "Amy's okay, I guess—I mean, for a girl. But she's always here. And when I'm at my dad's house she gets into my stuff."

Brian shot a quick glance at Ben to see how he was taking this, but when Ben remained silent he continued.

"It feels weird to be here, like I don't really belong. She *lives* here. I almost never get to see my mom and when I do, I have to share her with you guys. Dad doesn't even have a computer, so this is the only place I can play, and then Amy messes up my games. She knows she's not supposed to, but she does it anyway. I wish it was still just Mom and me—we never had problems then!"

Suddenly, for Ben, something clicked into place. Behind Brian's anger and temper he suddenly saw the displaced, confused boy he hadn't really noticed before. While he didn't like having his books thrown on the floor, and although Brian's attitude often provoked him, he realized that Brian's feelings made sense and that making progress in their relationship together would mean dealing with them.

"Come here for a moment, Brian, and sit by me," Ben said, walking over to the sofa in the corner. "Please?"

Brian looked reluctant but followed his stepfather. "I know you've been through a lot of changes lately, and I guess I haven't always understood how hard it was for you. I've felt confused and angry sometimes, and I bet Amy and your mom have, too."

Brian nodded.

"I'm sorry Amy ruined your computer game; we'll have to see what we can do about that. But what I really want to work on is helping you see that you do have a special place here, even if it's only on weekends. Your mom loves you, and I want to get to know you better. Think we can work on being friends?"

"I guess so," was all Brian had to say. But he accepted Ben's arm around his shoulders, and Ben noticed that from that day on, Brian seemed less angry and more willing to listen. Jody and Ben sat down with both children and did some brainstorming about respecting others' property—and about proper use of the computer. They also decided that Jody needed to spend at least part of each weekend that Brian visited alone with her son.

Ben was able to begin a new, more respectful relationship with his stepson because he practiced active listening: he noticed Brian's feelings and mirrored them back to him without judgment or criticism. Because Brian felt understood, he was more willing to listen to his stepfather and to work with him on solutions to the problem.

Notice that active listening does not require that you agree with feelings or that you accept poor behavior. It simply provides a foothold of understanding and respect so that the people you love and live with (both adults and children) feel heard and can move on to cooperation and problem solving. It also provides an opportunity to clarify those mysterious impulses known as feelings and to be sure you really do understand what's going on with your children and partner.

> Active listening does not require that you agree with feelings or that you accept poor behavior.

Ben gave Brian a great deal more than sympathy. By responding with active listening, he refrained from lecturing, nagging, or explaining and invited Brian to explore what was going on for him—and to share it with someone who could help him. Ben felt angry and frustrated by Brian's attitude, but he remembered that there could be a difference between what he felt and what he decided to do; he chose to focus on Brian's emotions and, in doing so, opened the door to real communication and understanding.

It's not enough to say, "I know how you feel." You may believe that you know what someone else feels, only to find out later that you were wrong. Be willing to spend time exploring children's feelings, and be careful not to take the feelings you uncover personally (which is often easier said than done). Avoid lecturing. Instead, ask questions designed not to trap or accuse but to show genuine curiosity. Say, "What else would you like me to know?" and "Is there anything else?" Ask for examples. And try hard not to deny feelings. "Well, that's a silly way to feel" is generally not helpful. It's better to say, "I believe I understand your feelings. Now, how do you think you could deal with them?"

You may want to assist children in finding ways to express their emotions. Angry children, for instance, can punch a "bop bag," smash and knead clay, or race to the corner and back. You may invite them to explore the feeling by giving it a name and asking them with genuine curiosity how it feels to them. Remember, young children especially have little experience with emotions and often have no words for them. Active listening can be an effective teaching tool. Whatever you and your children choose to do, validating feelings is an excellent beginning.

Using Positive Time-Out to Manage Strong Emotions

Q: Our three-year-old daughter was having a difficult time at her preschool. When the activities changed and she wanted to continue doing her own thing, she would lose her temper. She had tantrums at home, too, and her father and I were spending a lot of time yelling at her to stop. Her preschool teacher suggested something called a "positive time-out" to help her calm down. She had a cool-off spot at school and wanted to build one in her closet at home. So we did, and now she wants to stay there all the time. It does work—when she has a tantrum we ask her to take a cool-off, and she calms down on her own—but last night she wanted to sleep there (we let her). Is this okay?

A: Absolutely. Your daughter is learning the essential ability to "self-soothe," or to recognize and deal with her own feelings and to manage them. Many parents who try positive time-out with their children worry that it works almost too well, but their fears are usually related to the belief that children should be punished for poor behavior and a time-out that children enjoy doesn't feel like punishment. And it shouldn't.

Your daughter feels comfortable in her cool-off spot, which helps her calm down. There is a direct link between a child's feelings and her behavior, as you can see with your daughter: When she is calm, she is better able to get along, both at home and at school, and can choose more appropriate behavior. Most children don't actually want to sleep in their time-out spot, but it certainly does no harm!

Sometimes emotions are too overwhelming to handle, for adults and for children. Communication is a vital part of problem solving (and effective discipline), and feelings have a huge effect on your ability to communicate. Active listening is one way of working with feelings, but others are possible as well.

If you have little ones, you have undoubtedly witnessed the emotional thunderstorm known as a tantrum. Adults have tantrums, too—often in response to their children's! No one does his or her best work when angry, irritated, or out of control. In the same way that adults often do better when they take a moment to count to ten, take a deep breath, or leave the room for a moment, children, too, can get along better when they have help in recognizing and dealing with their emotions.

All human beings are born with the innate ability to self-soothe—to calm down, reduce stimulation, and manage difficult emotions. In fact, infants will break eye contact with their mothers when the level of stimulation rises too high, and some infant crying may actually be a way of releasing tension so the baby can relax.

Why talk about a discipline tool such as time-out in a chapter on feelings? It is a simple but powerful truth that most people *do* better when they *feel* better, and one way of helping children deal with their occasionally unruly emotions is by using positive time-out. Notice that this is not the punitive time-out so many parents rely on ("Stop that before I count to three, or you're in time-out!"). This time-out is intended to teach and to give children the opportunity to calm down *so that they can catch their breath, solve problems, and behave more appropriately.* This sort of time-out is often the first step on the path to effective communication.

Positive time-out works best with children who are older than two-and-a-half or three years of age. Find a place where your child feels comfortable and invite him to help you create a time-out spot. You may stack up cozy pillows, fold up a blanket, and add stuffed animals or favorite toys. Puzzles, story tapes, or koosh balls are often a welcome addition. Then, when your child has a tantrum or is out of sorts, he can go to his time-out spot and stay there as long as he needs to. When he returns, he should be able to choose better behavior; if not, he can return to his time-out spot. There is no timer, no "one minute for each year of your child's age." And no battle of wills over getting a child to *stay* in time-out.

If a child does resist the suggestion, "Would it help you if you went to your cool-off place?" you could offer, "Would you like me to go with you?" If there is still resistance, you could say, "Well then, I think I'll go." Why not? Maybe you need some cool-off time even more than your child does. If not, you are modeling that time-out truly can be a place to help one feel better in order to do better. At one time, we weren't sure how well positive time-out would work with older children, but we have found that it works very well *if* they are involved in the planning process.

> Because most people *do* better when they better, a way to help children deal with their occasionally unruly emotions is to use positive time-out.

Older children or teens may find it useful to listen to music, read quietly, or go outdoors to shoot baskets until they are calm. Then adults and children can settle down to deal with whatever issue they face—together, with respect and dignity. You and your children will undoubtedly find that you work more smoothly together when you can give each other room to accept feelings without being ruled by them and to manage them respectfully.

Practicing Emotional Honesty

"WELL," YOU MAY be wondering, "what about *my* feelings?" Parents and stepparents often wonder how much of their own feelings they should share with children—or with each other! It may be helpful to remember that, as with so many other things in life, children learn best by watching their adult role models. If you deal with anger by yelling, it shouldn't surprise you if your children yell, too. On the other hand, expressing what you feel in helpful ways will not only reduce the chance of conflict but will also provide children with a wonderful example of how to deal with emotions appropriately.

Emotional honesty may be the best policy. Children are unusually skillful at reading the energy of their parents' emotions, and when you are upset, it may be wise just to say, "I'm feeling really hurt right now." It isn't necessary to blame or shame, but it can be amazingly helpful for children to understand what you feel and why. Emotional honesty can save you and the children in your life a great deal of misunderstanding and confusion.

One helpful way of expressing your feelings is by using "I" statements—a simple formula that will help you know what to say, especially when you may be too upset to think straight. An "I" statement might look something like this:

"When you don't come home on time, I feel worried that something
  might have happened to you. I'd appreciate it if you could give me a
  call when you're going to be late."
"I feel angry and sad when it seems to me that my children are ignored
  while your children receive so much of your attention. I'd appreciate it
  if we could find ways to do things together."

As much as possible, offer the simple truth without details your listeners may not need to hear. For instance, "I'm angry at your dad right now" is a statement of fact. It's unnecessary (and hurtful) to add "because he's an inconsiderate jerk, and if you're not careful, you'll turn out just like him!" Stick to the facts; explain what you feel and, if appropriate, why you feel as you do. If that seems impossible, a time-out to cool down may be a good idea before you say anything at all.

> Expressing what you feel in helpful ways not only reduces the chance of conflict but also provides children with a wonderful example of how to deal with emotions appropriately.

Two points are the keys to the effective expression of emotional honesty. The first is to know that it is okay for you to think what you think, feel what you feel, and want what you want. The second is to understand that others may not think or feel the same way and that they are not obligated to give you what you want.

Some people have not learned to express their emotions honestly because they don't believe that what they think, feel, and want is okay. Others have trouble because they use emotional honesty as a way to control others; they believe that once someone knows what they think, feel, and want, that person should comply with their wishes. The former is disrespectful to self; the latter is disrespectful to others. Mutual respect is the key to successful relationships.

We Are in This Together

ACCORDING TO AN old saying, "the soul would have no rainbow had the eye no tear." Grief, loss, anger, and insecurity are a part of everyone's life—and so, lest we forget, are joy, serenity, and love. Emotions come with being human, and everything that happens in your family is not because you are a stepfamily. Remember to keep a realistic perspective: Tension and conflict can result from a number of different causes—not just your remarriage.

> Stick to the facts; explain what you feel and, if appropriate, why you feel as you do.

Financial stress, moving to a new home, losing a relative or a beloved pet—all sorts of things can cause upset and misunderstanding. The skills of active listening, self-soothing, and emotional honesty will serve you and your family well no matter what difficulties you may face. Exploring and respecting your children's and partner's feelings and being honest about your own will enable you to develop communication and relationship skills that will last a lifetime.

9

Family Meetings

The Foundation for Respect
and Problem Solving

WE'VE ALREADY MENTIONED family meetings several times in this book, and by now most people are at least somewhat familiar with the concept. There is, however, a huge difference between understanding something and making it part of everyday life. You may be more motivated to have family meetings when you realize that such meetings are among the most powerful tools available to stepfamilies (in fact, to any family) to create respect, understanding, and harmony.

Oh, we can easily find lots of "good" reasons not to have family meetings. You may wonder where on Earth you'll find time in your already complicated

schedule to do one more thing. Perhaps you have tried family meetings in the past, and they turned into organized gripe sessions that no one wanted to attend. Or perhaps certain members of your family think meetings are "dumb."

It's true that family meetings can feel awkward until everyone gets used to them, but they are well worth the effort. If what human beings need is to have a sense of belonging and to feel significant and worthwhile, there is no better place than the family meeting to create a spirit of teamwork, cooperation, and understanding. The family meeting also teaches children communication and problem-solving skills that will serve them in all aspects of their lives. Family meetings are helpful for all families, but they are essential for stepfamilies.

Long-Range Benefits of Family Meetings

THERE ARE MANY excellent reasons to begin holding family meetings. You may remember that one characteristic of healthy families is commitment; setting aside time regularly to gather your family together demonstrates commitment in a very practical way. Many people find that they keep appointments with business associates, friends, and even strangers but fail to reserve time for their own family—even when they know that many potential pitfalls exist in building a strong stepfamily. While family meetings may not solve every problem, they do provide a forum in which each member of your new family can feel heard and can play a part in helping the family function better. Family meetings are a wonderful way to draw on the observations, skills, humor, and creativity of each member of your family.

> There is no better place than the family meeting to create a spirit of teamwork, cooperation, and understanding.

Family meetings are an opportunity to create mutual respect through joint problem solving. As we've already seen, joining two families together can be a complicated task. Family meetings are a practical, realistic way of finding compromise, figuring out what works, and fine-tuning solutions. Meetings are also a time for conversation, staying in touch, and getting to know each adult and child in the family as the unique, special person he or she is.

Family meetings give children the chance to learn that their thoughts, feelings, and ideas are taken seriously and may provide adults with insights they might otherwise miss. What better way to build confidence, self-esteem, and mutual understanding? Last, but certainly not least, family meetings provide the opportunity to build a family tradition, create memories, and establish a family identity. For stepfamilies, family meetings are an invaluable part of life together.

Family Meetings—and Solutions—in Action

EACH STEPFAMILY IS unique. And just as families differ in their personalities, priorities, and problems, so family meetings—and the solutions they create—will differ. The following story, which appears in the revised edition of *Positive Discipline* (Jane Nelsen; Ballantine, 1996), is a wonderful example of how parents and children can work together.

> Just as families differ in their personalities, priorities, and problems, so family meetings—and the solutions they create—will differ.

When Jim and Betty married, each brought three children to their new family. The six children ranged in age from 6 to 14. Obviously, there were many adjustments to be made.

Betty was employed outside the home. She enjoyed her new family and was eager to get home to them after work—except for one problem. The first thing she noticed when she arrived home was the mess. The children would come home from school and leave their books, sweaters, and shoes all over the house. Then they would add cookie crumbs, empty milk glasses, and toys.

Betty would begin nagging and cajoling. "Why can't you pick up your things? You know it upsets me. I enjoy being with you, but I get so angry when I see all this mess that I forget about the joy." The children would then pick up their things, but by that time Betty was upset and displeased with them—and with herself.

Betty finally put the problem on the agenda for their weekly Monday night family meeting. She admitted that the problem was hers. It obviously didn't bother the children to have the house cluttered, but she asked for their help with her problem.

The children came up with a plan for a "safe-deposit box." This was to be a big cardboard box that they would put in the garage. The rule was that anything left in the common rooms—such as the living room, family room, and kitchen—could be picked up by anyone who saw it and put in the safe-deposit box. They also decided the item would have to stay there for a week before the owner could claim it.

> Family meetings provide the opportunity to build a family tradition, create memories, and establish a family identity.

The plan worked beautifully. The clutter problem was taken care of, and the safe-deposit box was jammed with things. However, some other problems arose that tested the plan. If the family had not been willing to stick to the rules they all agreed on, the whole arrangement would have been ineffective.

For instance, 12-year-old David lost his school shoes. He looked everywhere and then remembered the safe-deposit box. Sure enough, that is where they were. David wore his smelly old tennis shoes to school, but the next day he lost those. He didn't have any other shoes, but the other children insisted that he abide by the rules: He couldn't take his school shoes out of the safe-deposit box for a week.

David turned to Betty, who wisely said, "I'm sorry. I don't know what you are going to do, but I have to stick by the rules, too." His helpful siblings finally came up with the solution of wearing his bedroom slippers. David didn't have a better idea, so he wore his slippers to school for three days. After that week, he never left his shoes out again.

Then David's sister, 8-year-old Susan, lost her coat. It was difficult for Jim and Betty to stay out of these situations. After all, what kind of parents would let their children attend school in slippers and go coatless in cold weather? They decided to forget about what other people might think and let Susan handle the problem herself, as David had. Susan wore two sweaters to school for a week. (Betty made a friendly call to let the children's teachers know what was happening. If your family decides on a solution that affects children's appearance at school, letting teachers and principals know in advance may save everyone some misunderstanding and worry.)

Betty was astonished at how many of her own things disappeared into the safe-deposit box. She realized how much easier it was to notice clutter caused by others than to see her own. Jim also "lost" two ties, a sport coat, and several magazines.

This plan worked for this family because they followed these concepts:

- The problem was shared in a family meeting, and the children created the solution themselves.
- Jim and Betty did not step in to take responsibility when problems arose in carrying out the family's decision; instead, they empowered their children by expressing confidence in their ability to solve problems.
- The children enforced the rules because their parents stayed out of it.
- The rules applied to everyone in the family, including the adults.

How Do You "Do" Family Meetings?

REMEMBER, WHAT WORKS for one family won't necessarily work for another. After all, each family is different and has different needs and ideas. But keeping several points in mind will help you and your stepfamily have enjoyable and helpful family meetings:

1. Make family meetings a priority. Family meetings should be a priority and should happen at a regular, predictable time. Most families find it helpful to set aside the same time each week, preferably when no one must dash off to another activity. Don't allow yourself to be distracted by television or the telephone. Remember, you are sending a message that your new family is important.

2. Begin each meeting with compliments and appreciations. Take a moment to notice and share the positive things each family member has accomplished or experienced, and encourage everyone to do the same. This can be a tricky task for siblings (and stepsiblings) more accustomed to put-downs and criticism than compliments, but it's worth the effort. Taking the time to appreciate everyone in the family will get your meeting off to an encouraging start.

You may also enjoy creating a moment of togetherness to ease your family into "meeting mode." You might invite members of your family to take turns sharing a favorite cartoon or joke or to read a short quotation or story. The

STEPS TO SUCCESSFUL FAMILY MEETINGS

1. Make family meetings a priority.

2. Begin each meeting with compliments and appreciations.

3. Post an agenda sheet.

4. Respect all feelings and opinions.

5. Brainstorm for solutions and hold out for consensus.

6. Share responsibility at family meetings.

7. Have fun!

members of one family whose spiritual life was extremely important to them took turns sharing a Scripture and then opening their family meeting with a prayer. Whatever you choose, do your best to set a positive and encouraging mood. This is not the moment for complaints and hassles!

3. Post an "agenda sheet." Put an agenda sheet in a prominent place (the refrigerator seems to be a perennial favorite), and let family members know they can write down items to discuss at the next family meeting. Children too young to write may ask an older family member to write down their problems or ideas. Then be sure that each item on the agenda is discussed. Often just having a place to vent frustrations is enough, and by the time the meeting rolls around, the problem has been solved. If the problem still exists, the family will want to brainstorm together for solutions.

4. Respect all feelings and opinions. Problem solving should respect the feelings and opinions of each member of your family. If a problem involves children who are present only on weekends or vacations, it is both practical and respectful to have a family meeting when they are able to participate,

> Problem solving should respect the feelings and opinions of each member of your family.

even when this is not the "regular" time. When problems involve ex-partners or extended family (and your relationship is amicable enough), invite them to a family meeting to get their insights and suggestions. (Don't scoff! You might be surprised at what family meetings can accomplish.)

5. Brainstorm for solutions and hold out for consensus. Brainstorming is one way to create a sense of belonging, significance, and equality. Also, cooperation increases when everyone is involved in creating solutions.

Brainstorming means that all ideas are welcome (none are "stupid"). Appoint a "recorder" to list suggestions; don't evaluate suggestions until your brainstorming has run out of gas. Once everyone has had the chance to contribute his or her views, the family can decide together which suggestions will work best. If you question the value of a solution your family is considering, try asking "what" and "how" questions to assist them in seeing possible results or complications. For instance, "What do you think will happen if you do that?" is much more respectful than "Well, that's a silly idea!" As much as possible, work for consensus rather than taking a vote. Solutions work best when everyone involved agrees on what to do. When your family can't agree, just table the item until the next week and keep discussing it until consensus can be reached. Tabling items allows family members time to calm down and cool off. It also helps families learn how important it is to keep using the family meeting process until everyone feels satisfied.

You may be wondering, "Why can't we just take a vote?" Remember, part of the reason for having family meetings is to create cooperation and belonging. Voting creates winners—and losers. And the losers are unlikely to be highly motivated to cooperate. Working for consensus will give you far better results over the long term.

6. Share responsibility at family meetings. Let members of the family take turns being the chairperson and recorder. Once they've had some practice and training, children handle family meetings quite well and are often more motivated when they are trusted with some of the responsibility. Writing down suggestions and details will lessen the chance of misunderstanding later on.

7. Have fun! Remember the value of fun; end each family meeting with thanks and with plans for a fun family activity, a game, or a shared dessert.

Using Family Meetings to Create Routines

MUCH OF THE upheaval in stepfamilies comes from a lack of familiarity and routine. Everyone is new at living together, and often a way of doing things hasn't been established yet, or everyone did it differently "before." New partners may have different approaches to doing the laundry, mowing the lawn, or organizing kitchen drawers, along with children trained in their own approach; sometimes it's the ordinary and mundane tasks of family life that lead to the biggest hassles. Creating routines together is a great way to establish how things will be done in your new stepfamily, and there is no better place to create routines than in a family meeting.

Routines can be magic, especially with younger children. Older children can learn to create their own routine charts and learn good organizational skills. Clear expectations and predictable activities can help smooth the bumps out of a child's day, and once a routine is in place, it becomes the boss. Many families find that having a morning routine or a bedtime routine that is cozy and familiar makes everyone's life more pleasant.

Creating routines that work for your stepfamily may take some planning and experimentation, but they're worth the effort. Plan on doing some teaching so that children can take responsibility (and experience success) for appropriate parts of each activity. For instance, your evening routine might include making lunches, setting out clothes for the next morning, and making sure all schoolbooks and assignments are at hand. Bedtime may include brushing teeth, washing faces, putting on pajamas, saying prayers, and reading a story or singing a lullaby. Morning routines can include breakfast, clean-up, feeding pets, and getting off to school and work. Different ways of doing things can be approached as ways for the entire family to learn together. As children get older, they can do more and more of each routine themselves—although they'll always need you for a good night hug or smile!

Routines work best when children are involved in their creation. After deciding together what the routines will be, have fun making routine charts. Your children may want to draw pictures that represent each task or cut pictures from magazines. Glitter, markers, and stickers add to the fun. When children get distracted or defiant, let them check out what the boss has to say: "What is next on our routine chart?" Note that routine charts are not sticker or reward charts; they are simply a "map" showing children what comes next. Routines that are consistent and predictable can make family life run much more smoothly.

> Creating routines together is a great way to establish how things will be done in your new stepfamily.

Will Family Meetings Really Work?

MORNINGS IN THE Roberts' home were always a bit chaotic, but this morning was even louder than most. Liz looked up from the morning paper to see 11-year-old Jessica storming down the hall, closely followed by her same-age stepsister, Audrey.

"Mom," wailed Jessica, "I can't find my math book or my math homework sheet. I was going to do it this morning before school, but it's gone. She took them!" Jessica shot an angry glare at her stepsister, who rolled her eyes and glared at Liz.

"She lost her paper somewhere. And she always says I take her things, and you always take her side!" Audrey was angry now, too. "Jessica is careless with her stuff and she always accuses me when my dad is at work. There's never anyone to be on my side."

Liz gazed at the two girls and sighed. Life seemed so complicated these days. She and Jessica had moved into Brad's home when they married, and Brad's two children had had to give up a lot of their space. His son, Justin, had managed to keep his own room simply by virtue of being male, but the two girls had been forced to share Audrey's small bedroom. Even though they seemed to like each other reasonably well, arguments had been frequent. Liz found herself wondering whether she did indeed "always" take Jessica's side.

"I can see you're both pretty upset right now," Liz said quietly, "but we need to figure out what to do about this. Why don't you write the problem down on the agenda board, and we'll all talk about it together at the next family meeting? You'd better hurry—the bus will be here in a few minutes."

Jessica and Audrey grumbled, but they complied with Liz's request and headed out the door to school. Two days later the family gathered around the cleared-off kitchen table, and Brad called the meeting to order.

"Okay," he said with a smile, "who wants to begin with compliments and appreciations?" There was a moment of silence; Jessica and Audrey were still mad at each other and found saying anything positive a challenge. Liz gave 14-year-old Justin appreciation for having mowed the lawn without being asked. Brad then went down on one knee next to Liz's chair and thanked her for being the woman of his dreams and presented her with a yellow rose. He managed to look so ridiculous that both girls giggled. That broke the ice; more compliments followed, and the family relaxed and moved on to the items on the agenda.

"What's this about math books and homework?" Brad asked, looking over at Audrey. The story spilled out, along with both girls' frustration at having to share a room, be in the same class at school, compete for the attention of their friends, and be constantly in each other's company.

"Sounds pretty grim," Brad said sympathetically.

Jessica scrunched up her face, then looked at her stepsister. "Actually, Audrey's okay. Most of the time I really like her. But we get our stuff all mixed up, and it's hard to have any privacy around here. I can't even be alone with my friends. You guys just think we should get along all the time, but it's harder than you think," she finished.

"Yeah," Audrey chimed in.

Brad and Liz looked at each other, then at the girls. "I know it's been an adjustment for you two," Liz said. "And we appreciate that you've tried so hard to get along. Let's brainstorm some ideas and see what we can do to make things better."

The family spent about ten minutes brainstorming, laughing occasionally, and nodding at particularly good ideas. When they had finished, Brad asked Audrey to read the list of suggestions. Several ideas were good, and after some discussion the family decided on a few to try. The girls particularly liked Justin's suggestion that they replace their twin beds with bunk beds and use the additional space for two small desks and bookshelves, where they could keep their school supplies, assignments, and books separate. They also agreed to label drawers and baskets in the closet in which to keep their clothing and laundry.

Audrey and Jessica both agreed to help with extra family chores and contribute allowance money to help with the cost of the new furniture. Brad and Liz agreed to listen carefully when the girls had a problem and to work on not taking the side of their birth child. "That'll take some practice," Liz admitted ruefully. "Can you guys help me remember?"

Jessica and Audrey nodded.

"Can we have a snack now?" Audrey asked.

"We had a snack last meeting. We should play a game this time," Jessica said quickly. The girls glared at each other, then looked at Liz. She opened her mouth to speak, then shut it again and clapped her hand over it dramatically.

Everyone laughed. The girls looked at each other a bit sheepishly, then Jessica spoke. "I guess we could have snacks *and* a game," she said. "Okay with everybody?"

Her solution was greeted with smiles, and the family meeting was adjourned.

Not every problem that faces your blended family requires a family meeting, but family meetings are wonderful places to teach children important life skills. They do provide a time and place for family members to listen to each other, recognize each other's accomplishments and contributions, and learn to work together to find mutually acceptable solutions to the inevitable controversies of daily life.

Your meetings will undoubtedly feel a bit awkward at first—most new things do. For stepfamilies, for whom everything can seem new and strange, family meetings are an efficient and enjoyable way to speed the process of learning to live together as a family, build closeness and trust, and create a welcoming home that each member can feel a part of.

10

Building Belonging

The Magic of Encouragement

WOULDN'T IT BE wonderful if there were a way to prevent misbehavior, build trust and understanding, and develop confidence and self-esteem in your children? Would you believe us if we told you there is such a way? You may not be able to completely prevent misbehavior, but you can learn to understand what misbehavior means and how to deal with it in encouraging ways. You can learn to look beyond behavior for the "hidden message," the belief behind the behavior. You can learn to understand which behaviors are based on mistaken conclusions about how to belong (which does not mean you do nothing about them). When you have this perspective—this understanding of what behavior is about—you can handle situations rationally and lovingly. You can begin to see every problem as a learning opportunity, for you and your children.

One of the most effective tools in Positive Discipline may not seem like discipline at all, but it has a powerful influence on how your children behave. The tool we are talking about is encouragement, which means "to gladden the heart." We have learned that all of us—especially children—need to develop a sense of belonging and significance. This is what encouragement is all about. Not surprisingly, human beings usually do better when they feel better, and believing that you are worthwhile and can make a positive contribution and be appreciated for who you are encourages you to do your best in life.

For children, becoming part of a stepfamily (along with all the change that process may entail) can disrupt that sense of belonging. While some children welcome their stepparents and thrive in their new family, others feel confused, dethroned, and displaced. It should not be surprising that children's behavior often reflects their feelings.

Learning to live together in a stepfamily can be tough work for everyone, and most people make mistakes along the way. We have said it before (and will undoubtedly say it again): Mistakes are wonderful opportunities to learn. When you can give yourself and those you love room to grow and learn, trust one another to go on loving, and laugh together occasionally, you can survive just about anything.

> When you give yourself and those you love room to grow and learn, trust one another to go on loving, and laugh together occasionally, you can survive just about anything.

Learning how to encourage is one of the most important tools of effective parenting—and stepparenting! Encouragement builds the attitudes and skills on which self-esteem depends, and those who study human development tell us that these abilities are among the greatest assets a child can have. Children who have learned to value and respect themselves and who have been taught to cope with even the difficult parts of life can take risks, accept new challenges, and deal with change.

Self-Esteem: What Is It, Anyway?

YOU MAY HAVE heard someone say, "I don't have much self-esteem." (You may have even said so yourself!) Self-esteem has become something of a buzzword in our society. You're supposed to be able to "get" it somehow and "give" it to your children. And when you do, you're magically immune from having bad days, being depressed, or feeling discouraged. Right?

Well, not exactly. Self-esteem is an illusory notion. Have you ever noticed that when you have a good day, self-esteem seems to follow, yet when you have a bad day, your self-esteem goes down the tubes? So, is your self-esteem really the cause? Well, yes. Even the healthiest sense of self-esteem comes and goes as circumstance changes. Therefore, what children need are the abilities and skills to create healthy self-esteem more often and the resiliency to deal with situations when that self-esteem falters. True self-esteem allows you to learn from mistakes instead of thinking you are worthwhile only when you are perfect.

Self-esteem means accepting yourself and being able to recognize both your assets and your liabilities. It means being comfortable with who you are. And it means having an innate sense of worth that allows you to accept frustration, disappointment, or even failure and know you can survive.

Children cannot be "given" a healthy sense of self-esteem. Smiley faces on math papers, empty praise, and soccer leagues where everyone gets a trophy, win or lose, do not create self-esteem. Children must *grow* their own self-esteem through the skills and attitudes they learn—they grow it through life experience. When parents offer encouragement, effective discipline, and active listening, they are helping their children develop this powerful attribute. When parents can support their children through difficult experiences rather than trying to protect them from all pain, they are helping their children learn the inner strength they will need to be successful, capable adults.

Unfortunately, American culture doesn't always allow children to feel good about who they are. The advertising industry spends billions of dollars each year to convince us—and especially our young people—that to belong they must look good, be smart and sophisticated (and being sophisticated these days may mean drug use, smoking, or premature sexuality), be thin and attractive, and possess all the "right" things—the "right" athletic shoes, brand-name clothing, and accessories, or even the "right" toys and electronic gadgets.

Parents often overemphasize grades and achievement. We are not saying that grades and achievement are not important. But problems may begin when children believe that parents value grades and achievement over happiness and a sense of belonging and significance, or that parents are more interested in academic achievement than in the life choices that are important to their children. How can children develop a sense of belonging when they believe their parents' love is conditional?

> True self-esteem allows you to learn from mistakes instead of thinking you are worthwhile only when you are perfect.

Remember, self-esteem grows from a sense of belonging and significance; from the belief that you are capable, acceptable, and worthwhile; and from the ability to face challenges in life. Becoming part of a stepfamily may cause children to question whether they are "good enough" and where they fit in this new family arrangement. Combined with the pressures young people already face at school and from their peers, the results can be devastating. Children who do not feel a sense of belonging in their families will look for it elsewhere, and the cost of fitting in with their peers (which often means following the crowd) can be high for children, especially older children and adolescents. How can you help your children—those born to you and those who have arrived with your new partner—to believe in themselves, do their best, and be capable, happy people? How do you let them know they belong and are significant to you?

Accepting the Children You Have

THE BIRTH OF a child is a gift, one of the most wonderful things a person can experience. When a baby is born, that baby's parents almost always have dreams, hopes, and expectations. This child, they may think, will be a star football player, a great scholar, or a brilliant musician. It can come as something of a shock to discover that your children have their own dreams, hopes, and expectations; they have their own personalities, temperaments, and priorities. Eventually most parents accept that children must discover and follow their own paths in life. Helping children discover their unique strengths and potential is one of the great adventures of parenting.

For stepparents, this adventure can be especially challenging. Many stepparents find they have acquired children with whom they have little in common. Their stepchildren may have grown up in a different environment with an entirely different style of parenting. The children's perception of life, their opinions, their behavior, their goals—all can be very different from what the adult has experienced with his or her birth children.

It can be tempting—and, for better or worse, it's often human nature—to focus on what's *wrong*. Most people point out differences; they want things (and people) to be familiar and comfortable—to be "their" way. And it takes time to get to know and feel comfortable with people whose interests and lifestyle may differ from their own. Both adults and children in a stepfamily may feel they are "different," and, unfortunately, "different" sometimes ends up feeling like "less than."

> Helping children discover their unique strengths and potential is one of the great adventures of parenting.

Looking for the Positive

"SARAH! IT IS you! I haven't seen you in ages!" Sarah looked up at the sound of her name and saw Jenny, an old friend, coming toward her across the café, a big smile on her face. The two women hugged and were exchanging details of the past few years when Jenny took a step backward and looked more closely at her friend's face.

"You look tired, Sarah," she said. "Hasn't life been treating you well?"

Sarah smiled wearily. "If you want to hear about it, you'd better sit down," she said, gesturing toward her table. "It's a long story."

The two women gathered cups of steaming coffee and muffins and settled in for a long chat.

"You may have heard that I married Scott last year," Sarah began.

Jenny smiled. "I did hear that. Good for you—I always thought the two of you would be good together."

"We're fine. At least, I think we are. But Scott's daughter is another matter," Sarah said with a sigh.

"Why?" Jenny asked, puzzled. "Angela was always such a sweet kid. She and my girls used to hang out together. How old is she now—about 16?"

"That's right. She's a year older than my daughter, Grace. But boy, is she different. We seem to argue all of the time. I thought Grace and Angela would enjoy being sisters, but they hardly speak to each other. And Angela is so hard to get along with; she's sullen and depressed all the time, and she never wants to help out around the house. I've offered to take her to soccer or basketball with Grace, but she refuses; she just sits in her room. She has a notebook she's always scribbling in but she won't let her father or me see it. She just listens to sad music and avoids the rest of us. Just having her in the house is enough to depress me," Sarah finished with a grimace.

Jenny took a sip of her coffee before answering. "You know," she said quietly, "I remember Angela before her mother died. She was in my Girl Scout troop."

Sarah looked interested. "I'd forgotten that. Scott doesn't like to talk about Angela's mother. It seems to make him so sad. And Angela never speaks about her at all."

"Angela and her mom were very close," Jenny said. "They came to all the meetings together, and they always seemed to be laughing and hugging. But what I remember about Angela is her music."

"Her music?" Sarah looked puzzled. "You mean, what she listens to on her stereo?"

Now Jenny looked puzzled. "No, the music she played. Angela is a gifted pianist. Her mother was, too; in fact, they played duets together for us from time to time. Angela was planning to go back East somewhere to study. Are you saying she doesn't play anymore?"

"I didn't know she ever had," Sarah said slowly. "How could I not have known something like that?"

Jenny gazed thoughtfully at her friend. "I'm not sure, but maybe the music was too painful a reminder for Angela and Scott. It would be a shame if she gave it up, though."

"It certainly would." Sarah finished her coffee and smiled. "I have an idea," she said. "Maybe there's a way I can help Angela—and all of us—to feel a little more comfortable in our family."

It was a couple of days before Sarah had an opportunity to put her plan into action. The next time she heard the soft strains of music coming from Angela's room, she tapped lightly on the door.

"What is it?" Angela said.

"Can I come in for a minute?" Sarah asked.

"If you want to," came the unenthusiastic reply.

Sarah opened the door. Angela was putting her notebook in a drawer and looked at her stepmother uneasily. Sarah realized that the soft, sad music was classical music—some sort of slow piano piece.

"That's beautiful music," she said, sitting down on the edge of the bed.

"You don't know anything about it," Angela responded defensively.

Sarah bit back the harsh words that came to her lips and took a breath. "You're right," she said calmly. "But I'd like to. I didn't know you liked classical music."

"There's a lot about me you don't know," Angela said bitterly.

"I know that, too, Angela."

Angela looked into Sarah's face for the first time.

"I ran into Jenny Carter the other day—remember your old Girl Scout leader? She was asking how you were coming with your piano, and I had to tell her I didn't even know you played. Honey, I know we haven't been getting along, and I've realized that I expected you to be just like Grace, into sports and boys. After all, she's the only teenage girl I really know," Sarah said with a smile. "But you're a different sort of person, and I haven't taken the time to learn all the special things about you. Would you be willing to help me learn?"

Angela stood silently for a moment, chewing on her lower lip. Then she sighed and sat down beside her stepmother. "The piano is the most important thing in my life. Or at least it used to be. But when Mom died, Dad sold our piano. He said he couldn't bear to hear me play because it reminded him too much of her. At first I didn't mind because it made me sad, too. But now I miss it so much. Music is what I'm best at. Grace is so good at all the stuff she does, but I'm not. I wish I had my piano back; I wish Dad understood. I just feel angry and sad all the time. You must hate having me here."

Sarah remembered how harshly she'd described Angela to Jenny. "I don't understand you, Angela, but I really want to. I think we need to talk to your dad about your music, maybe even see about getting you a piano. You don't have to be like Grace, honey. You just have to be you. Do you think you'll be able to remember the pieces you knew? What happened to all your music?"

Angela hesitated and then impulsively went to the drawer and pulled out her notebook. "I have them all written in here," she said, opening the pages. "I wrote down all the pieces I knew and all the things Mom and I played together so I wouldn't ever forget." She looked quickly at her stepmother, then continued.

"I write down my memories of my mom. And I write poetry sometimes when I'm sad or lonely."

Sarah gazed down at the pages open before her and realized she was being offered a glimpse of her stepdaughter's heart. She saw the names of Chopin, Mozart, and Beethoven and grinned. "I know more about Led Zeppelin and the Beatles than I do about these composers," she said. "You'll have to teach me."

Sarah looked down just as Angela looked up and their eyes met. Suddenly Angela had her head buried in Sarah's shoulder, and Sarah realized she was weeping.

"It's okay, honey," she said soothingly, putting an arm around Angela's shoulders. "It's going to be okay now. No one wants you to forget your mother.

BECOMING A "GOOD FINDING" FAMILY

1. Identify the positives.

2. Give and encourage compliments.

3. Help children become "good finders."

4. Build on strengths.

And we need to help you find ways to be yourself. Let's talk to your dad tonight, shall we?"

It would take Angela and Sarah (and Scott and Grace) some time to find new ways to relate to one another. But Sarah made a conscious decision that instead of looking for the things that made Angela difficult and depressing, she would begin looking for the things that made Angela special. When she looked, she found more than she had expected.

Angela proved to be a sensitive, talented young woman. When her unique qualities were recognized and accepted, she began to open up and to spend more time with the rest of her new family. She and Grace discovered that they could appreciate each other's different strengths without having to share them. And Angela and her father found that while remembering her mother could sometimes be painful, it also brought back happy memories to them both and helped them strengthen their own relationship.

Like all of us, Angela possessed both assets and liabilities. She could still be moody and distant, but Sarah and Scott found that those times happened far less often than before. When Angela felt accepted and learned that she could be appreciated for just who she was, her attitude and mood improved.

Becoming "Good Finders"

PERHAPS IT'S A result of too much to do in too little time, but most parents are good at pointing out the chores that have not been done, the grade that was not acceptable, or the personality traits that are not pleasant. But what about all the things that have been done? What are the things that make your children (and your stepchildren) special and lovable? Have you told them lately what you appreciate about them?

People who thrive in relationships (and in life) tend to be "good finders." That is, they are skilled at finding what is good about those around them, and they are quick to point those things out. Perhaps nothing else is so powerful in changing the atmosphere and attitude in a family.

How does one become a good finder? Here's how:

1. Identify the positives. Take a quiet moment sometime soon, and sit down with several note cards or pieces of paper. Label each one with the name of a member of your family. Now list as many good qualities, talents, and positive things about each person as you can think of. You will probably discover that this is easy with some people and more difficult with others; if you do, you're normal! Keep your cards handy; add to them daily as you notice new things. How does looking for the positive affect your opinion of each person? Your relationship?

2. Give and encourage compliments. At least once each day, compliment each person in your family, using your list of positive qualities as a guide. Don't gush or be insincere, but let those around you know that you notice and appreciate the helpful things they do (even if you wish they would do more) and the qualities that make them special.

> People who thrive in relationships tend to be "good finders"— they are skilled at finding what is good about those around them, and they are quick to point those things out.

Expressing compliments may feel awkward at first. Most folks are more skilled at giving and receiving criticism than at giving and receiving compliments. Trust us: It gets easier with practice. Remember, this is not a time for criticism or problem solving; this is simply a time to appreciate and encourage.

3. Help your children become "good finders." Let your children know that successful, happy people are usually excellent good finders. Help them learn to be good finders, too. What things do they like about their family members (both in your home and their other parent's, if appropriate)? Use active listening to validate negative feelings, but try to focus on what's *right*. Because children (like their parents) are more used to focusing on what's wrong, becoming good finders will take some practice. It's well worth the effort. How do you think the atmosphere in your home might change if everyone became an accomplished good finder?

4. Build on strengths. What are your children good at? What do they most enjoy doing? All of us need ways to feel special, and all of us have innate abilities and talents that can help us find our own unique place in the world. One problem with being young is that children simply haven't yet had enough time to figure out what those talents and abilities are!

Teach children to manage their weaknesses and build on their strengths. The book *Soar with Your Strengths,* by Donald O. Clifton and Paula Nelson (Dell, 1992), begins with a delightful parable about a duck, a fish, an eagle, an owl, a squirrel, and a rabbit who attended a school with a curriculum that included running, swimming, tree climbing, jumping, and flying. Of course, all of the animals have strength in at least one of these areas but are doomed to fail in other areas. It is sobering to read about the punishment and discouragement these animals encounter when parents and school personnel insist they must do well in every area to "graduate" and become well-rounded animals. A major point of the book is that "excellence can be achieved only by focusing on strengths and managing weaknesses, not through the elimination of weakness"—an excellent lesson for all of us!

> Most folks are more skilled at giving and receiving criticism than at giving and receiving compliments.

Teach your children to manage their weaknesses and soar with their strengths. Ironically, children may learn mediocrity when their parents insist they try to earn all A's. Sometimes parents even penalize children by taking away the time they spend on their best subjects (where they feel encouraged) until they do better in their weak areas (where they feel discouraged). Instead, parents could coach their children to spend enough time on their weak areas to get by and devote most of their time to building on their strengths.

Some young people seem to know from birth what their destiny is; others grope and struggle for a way to fit in. Wise and caring adults can help children (and each other) find their strengths and create ways to build on them. Remember that intelligence and talent come in many different forms. Allow children to experiment. As much as is possible and appropriate, let them try new activities. Give them a chance to experience drama, sports, music, or dance. Encourage reading; make time for them to use the computer. When you and your children discover something they enjoy and are good at, build on it!

You will probably want to reach an agreement with your children about expectations for new activities. For example, if one child decides to try drum lessons, is it okay to quit if he or she doesn't like it? How soon? Do all members of your stepfamily have an equal opportunity to participate in activities?

Remember, too, that children need time just to hang out and play and to keep up with school and family work. But having something that makes him or her feel "special" can be a tremendous gift for a young person. Parents and stepparents can be helpers on a child's voyage of self-discovery.

Take Time to Teach

JIMMY, 11, WAS delighted when Pete, his stepfather, asked him to mow the front lawn. He'd been eager to get his hands on the new power mower, and he listened attentively as his stepdad told him briefly how to start the big machine. An hour later, sweaty but satisfied, he called Pete out to inspect the lawn. Unfortunately, the experience didn't turn out well for either of them.

Pete found lots of places Jimmy had missed, strips and spots of long grass, edges left untrimmed. The more of these he pointed out, the more unhappy and defensive Jimmy grew. Finally, in a burst of temper, Jimmy said, "Fine! See if I ever mow your old lawn again!"

Frustrated and annoyed, Pete retorted, "See if I ever ask you!" Neither would speak to the other for the remainder of that day.

> Teach your children to manage their weaknesses and soar with their strengths.

Cindy was getting ready to entertain friends for dinner, and Marie, five, had been pestering her mom all day long. "Let me help, Mommy," she said. "Let me do it!" At last Cindy gave in.

"Okay, sweetie," Cindy said. "Why don't you set the table for dinner? I've already put on the tablecloth; you just need to do the napkins and silverware."

Marie skipped happily off to help her mother. She spent a long time counting out knives and forks and napkins and placing them carefully on the table. But five-year-old hands are small, and neatness is a virtue that takes more than five years to develop. When Cindy finally had a moment to inspect the table, she discovered unfolded napkins and mismatched silverware. In an effort to be extra helpful, Marie had added dishes to the table, but she'd chosen the everyday plates instead of the "good" ones. With a shake of her head, Cindy went to work straightening things up.

When Marie wandered in later looking for her mom, she discovered an elegantly set table, every item neatly aligned. There was no trace of her slightly askew handiwork. Obviously, Marie thought, her work had not been good enough—Mom had to fix it. Next time Cindy wants Marie's help, she may get a different, less willing response.

Both Marie and Jimmy wanted to be helpful; they were enthusiastic about cooperating and working. What they lacked was size, maturity—and basic skills. It is encouraging to tackle a new job, as long as you have a fair chance at success. It is discouraging to do your best and discover it's not good enough. Jimmy's stepfather and Marie's mother gave neatness and perfection priority over encouraging and teaching their children. Is the lawn really more important than Jimmy's feelings or is a neat table setting more important than Marie's feelings?

> Encouragement doesn't cost money; it just takes patience, commitment, and a smile.

Jimmy's stepfather could have been encouraging by saying, "Thanks Jimmy. I appreciate your enthusiastic help. You tackled a very big job. Let's look at the lawn together so we can see what you did well and what might be done even better next time. I have faith in your judgment. How about if I point out all the good things, and you tell me what needs improvement?"

Encouragement doesn't mean accepting a sloppy job, but there are ways to be respectful while focusing on the good points and involving the child in

FOUR STEPS TO TEACHING A SKILL

1. Let her watch you.

2. You do it with her help.

3. She does it with your help.

4. You watch her.

evaluating what needs improvement. Marie's mother could have been more encouraging by accepting the job her daughter did and telling her friends about her daughter's desire to help and contribute. It is our guess that Cindy's friends would have been more entertained and impressed by Marie's contribution than by a perfectly set table. Later on, Cindy could take time to teach Marie another way to set the table.

> Taking time to teach is one of the most encouraging things an adult can do for a child.

Taking time to teach is one of the most encouraging things an adult can do for a child. Teaching not only helps children develop the skills and abilities to succeed (an essential part of developing self-esteem) but also can provide us with opportunities to know our children (and stepchildren) better and to enjoy closeness and even fun. Teaching is not as difficult as it sometimes seems.

1. Let her watch you. As your pupil watches you mow the lawn, set the table, or perform some other task, explain in simple terms what you are doing and why.

2. You do it with her help. Invite your child to work alongside you. Remind her of the things you told her before and let her know you welcome her help. (Whenever possible, use "what" questions to guide the process, such as "What things will you need to do _____?")

3. She does it with your help. Let your child try her hand at the task; your role is to provide occasional hints and help, as well as lots of encouragement.

4. You watch her. Now it's time to celebrate as your child accomplishes the task all by herself!

Remember, keep your expectations and standards realistic. Most people take a while to learn new things; children are no different. Remember, too, that life in a stepfamily takes some getting used to. Food, chores, and expectations may be handled very differently by a child's parent and stepparent. Teaching, along with lots of encouragement, will help ease all of you into your new family.

Mistakes Are Opportunities to Learn

NONE OF US will ever be perfect. Neither will our children or our partner's children. Sometimes we even may wonder whether we will ever live peacefully together, let alone love one another. Making room for mistakes can help everyone relax. Mistakes truly can be opportunities to learn and grow; when the messes have been cleaned up and the smoke has cleared, we can sit down together and do some learning. What needs to be different next time? How can we get a different result?

Creating an encouraging atmosphere can make your stepfamily a pleasant place for everyone. Encouragement doesn't cost money; it just takes patience, commitment, and a smile. Here are some encouraging things to try with the children and stepchildren in your life:

> Keep your expectations and standards realistic. Most people take a while to learn new things; children are no different.

- Give hugs for no reason.
- Listen attentively and accept children's feelings.
- Give opportunities to try new things; provide teaching to bring about success.
- Develop an "attitude of gratitude"—give compliments and appreciations regularly.

- Practice having faith in your children; say, "I believe you can learn to do that!"
- Celebrate successes, even little ones!
- Smile often.

It's true: People (little ones and big ones) do better when they feel better. Encouragement nourishes children and helps them believe they belong and can succeed, and encouraged children behave better. Wouldn't we rather avoid misbehavior than have to deal with it later?

11

Getting (and Staying) Connected

Building Strong Relationships with Kids

YOU MAY BE thinking that forging bonds of respect and affection is a task faced only by stepparents and their stepchildren. But in this hectic world of ours, there is no guarantee that even the most loving of birth parents is truly connected to his or her children. Encouragement, active listening, understanding loyalties, looking for the positives, and teaching skills are important parts of creating a healthy stepfamily. But they may not be enough.

Positive, effective discipline is important, too—and we'll spend time understanding what it is and how to use it in chapters 13 and 14. But tragic and sobering events like the shootings at Columbine High School and elsewhere around the nation have made parents stop and consider what is happening between them and the young people they love. In fact, if such horrible tragedies can be said to have a silver lining, perhaps that lesson is it.

Parents and children have always had moments when they struggled to understand and accept each other. But in slower, simpler times, the job seemed easier. These days, most parents and stepparents work outside the home. They are likely to return in the evening to a home where children have school assignments, sports, and other activities of their own and where an average of thirty-five hours per week

> Connecting with children—getting into their world and knowing the people they are becoming—takes conscious effort and time.

of domestic duties remain to be done. Technology intrudes. For many families, "quality time" means the family is at home, but each person is watching a separate television or computer screen, often in different rooms.

Adults feel a tremendous amount of stress; life moves too quickly, and children grow up too soon. Relaxing together around the dinner table has become a thing of the past for many families, and our relationships suffer because of it. Today, connecting with our children—truly getting into their world and knowing the people they are becoming—takes conscious effort. More important, it takes time. There simply are no shortcuts to effective parenting and happy, healthy relationships.

Getting into Your Child's World

MANY ADULTS WONDER from time to time whether their children's behavior is "normal" and why they think the way they do. Stepparents, particularly those who have never had children of their own, may find these questions especially puzzling. One important aspect of understanding children's behavior is having adequate information about physical, cognitive, and emotional development; children and teens truly do function and perceive the world differently than do adults. Another factor is learning to understand your child's unique temperament and personality. A number of excellent books deal with these subjects; we particularly recommend *Positive Discipline: The First Three Years* (Nelsen, Erwin, and Duffy, Prima, 1998), *Positive Discipline for Preschoolers, Revised Second Edition* (Nelsen, Erwin, and Duffy, Prima, 1998), and *Positive Discipline for Teenagers, Revised Second Edition* (Nelsen and Lott, Prima, 2000).

> Understanding children's behavior requires having adequate information about physical, cognitive, and emotional development.

Knowledge is essential. But each child is unique, a miraculous blend of genes, nurturing, and the individual essence we call a spirit or soul; a child can never be fully understood from any book, no matter how good. If you are living with stepchildren, you may find yourself feeling baffled by their behavior and perspective on the world. If you have children of your own, you may wonder how each one can be so different. And no matter what sort of parent you are, "step" or birth, you undoubtedly feel concern about who the children you live with are becoming, what their values are, and what they do when you aren't there to watch. If you haven't yet considered your children in this light, just wait until the day they drive away with their friends, leaving you to wonder what they're *really* up to!

It's far more important to know *who* your children are than just *where* your children are. But how can you build a close and lasting relationship with your children and stepchildren? Is there any way to keep them safe in this perilous world? How do you create a home where children see parents (and stepparents) as people to be trusted, as resources and respected allies rather than adversaries?

Staying Connected with Children

BUILDING A CONNECTION with the young people in your life can be done in any number of ways. It's worth saying, however, that all of them require an investment of something precious: time. "I don't have time" has become the lament of far too many American parents, so a word of caution is in order: You cannot be an effective parent or stepparent, and you can't build trust and understanding between you and your children, without spending time—lots of it. Spending time with your children is far more important than spending money on your children.

Too many young people these days report feeling "invisible"; they say their parents have too many things to do, are too busy to be with them, and don't seem to care about the things that matter to their children. Many parents buy parenting book after parenting book looking for the "magic wand" of child rearing, *the* approach that will guarantee them happy, well-behaved children. There is no such thing. As authors, we would love to offer you a warranty with this book, but even the most effective parenting tools require time, patience, and repetition—and there are no guarantees. If you're willing to invest your time and energy (and you probably wouldn't be reading this book if you weren't), the

> It's far more important to know *who* your children are than just *where* your children are.

following are some ways to build a strong connection with your children and stepchildren.

1. Spend "special time." As we will see when we examine the mistaken goals of behavior, a great deal of children's poor behavior is intended to attract adult attention. The tragedy of misbehavior is that it works so well: Adults invariably pay lots of attention when children are behaving badly. (Some children, in fact, become convinced that the *only* way to get attention is to behave badly.) A simple but effective way of creating a sense of belonging (and avoiding misbehavior) is to spend "special time" with a child. Special time is also one of the best ways to truly know and understand the person your child is becoming.

Special time means one-on-one time that you spend with each child in your family. It need not be hours and hours; ten or fifteen minutes on a regular basis may be enough. Nor do you need to spend money on elaborate activities or entertainment. Special time is time you devote to just being with your child, listening, hanging out, and doing things together. The gift of your time is almost always the best way to tell a child "You matter to me."

STEPS TO CONNECTING WITH KIDS

1. Spend "special time."

2. Choose curiosity over judgment.

3. Explore the world of play.

4. Be aware of the influence of technology and culture.

5. Share your own history.

6. Use discipline to teach and guide.

7. Be patient.

One busy mom decided to take each child in her family in turn to run errands and do the shopping while her husband remained at home with the others. She discovered that an hour or so chatting while they drove and shopped was a marvelous way to stay in touch with each child. Her husband also set aside a time of his own to spend with the children. Another family created a "special time" calendar that showed when each child would have time alone with each parent; the children also brainstormed for ways they could stay occupied while it was their sibling's turn, knowing that their special time would come.

There are many ways of creating one-on-one time with your children. You may invite your family's help at a family meeting to discover ways to spend special time, or you may pause during each day to enjoy the moments that come along. Budgeting time, however, is much like budgeting money: If you don't plan for expenses, they may not be possible! Making special time a priority in your schedule may make a big difference in the way your family feels to all of you.

2. Choose curiosity over judgment. Margaret knocked on her son's bedroom door, then realized from the vibrating wood and booming bass that he couldn't hear her. Alex, 14, had his favorite hip-hop music turned up as loud as it would go—again.

"Turn that down!" Margaret shouted, as she opened the door. "Dinner's ready! Why must you have that up so loud? I don't know how you can listen to it—it's obscene," she finished grumpily, then felt a twinge of guilt as she saw the hurt in Alex's eyes.

"What's up, Meg?" her husband Mark asked as she stalked back into the kitchen.

"Alex is listening to that rap stuff again," she said. "I hate it—the language is awful and it glorifies crime. I don't like the way it talks about women, either. I've thought about forbidding him to listen to it, but all of his friends do; he'll just listen when he's with them. I know he's a good kid, but why does he like such horrible music?"

Mark grinned. "That's how our folks used to feel about the Beatles and the Rolling Stones, remember? And how their folks felt about Frank Sinatra. Or the way older people felt about the waltz back in Vienna when it first arrived. Scandalous!" He reached out and gave his wife a squeeze. "Have you ever talked calmly with Alex about it?"

Margaret shook her head sheepishly. "No, I just lecture and nag him about it. He's lucky to have a stepdad like you, honey. I'd probably drive him crazy all by myself."

Several days later, Margaret was driving home from the mall with Alex, who had used his birthday money to buy a new CD. "You know, Alex," Meg said thoughtfully, "I've been pretty hard on you about your music. And I'm wondering why you like rap—or is it hip-hop?—so much. Could you put your new CD on the car player and maybe explain it to me?"

"Are you crazy, Mom?" Alex blurted out. Then, more softly, "You know you hate my music. Besides, it has the 'f' word in it."

> The gift of your time is almost always the best way to tell a child "You matter to me."

"I've heard that word before," Margaret said with a laugh. "Just be sure you don't ever say it to me! Anyway, I want to understand you, Alex. When I was your age, my parents complained about my music, but they would never actually listen to it. It used to make me mad. I guess I don't want to treat you the same way. Why don't you play the tune you like the best?"

"Well, okay," Alex said uncertainly. "But you won't like it."

He was right: Margaret didn't. But as they listened, she asked Alex to explain to her what things he liked about the music and about that particular artist. She asked him how the music made him feel. And she listened carefully to his answers. On the way home from the mall, Meg and her son had a fascinating and wide-ranging conversation about prejudice, race, attitudes toward women, drugs, and teen behavior.

As they pulled into the driveway and Alex removed his CD, he looked over at his mother. "Mom, I hope you know that just because I listen to this music, I'm not going to go out and do drugs or something. I just like the beat. And I know the difference between right and wrong."

"I know you do, Alex. Thank you for sharing your music with me. I learned a lot."

A few days later, Alex presented his mother with a special gift. Looking just a little embarrassed, he handed her a CD with a hand-lettered label. "I made this for you on Dad's CD burner when I was at his house last weekend," he said. "It's some of my favorite music for you to have."

Margaret took the CD and gave Alex a hug, recognizing that he had offered her a place in his heart and life. "Thanks," she said, meaning it sincerely. "This means a lot to me."

Will Margaret ever truly love hip-hop music? Probably not. But by showing curiosity about her son's interest rather than judging it, she was able to open a door between them. What could have become an issue that divided them became instead a way to communicate and connect.

Most parents love their children so much that they worry about what their tastes, behaviors, and ideas might mean for their future. It's tempting to condemn and criticize what you fear or don't understand, and sometimes there are good reasons to be concerned. Margaret was able to get past her worry and distaste by showing genuine curiosity, by asking Alex "what" and "how" questions, and by being willing to really listen to his answers. She now has a way to stay in tune with Alex and to check from time to time about how he's doing and what he's thinking. Moreover, discipline, should it be needed, is almost always more effective when built on a foundation of real understanding and respect.

> "**W**hat" and "how" questions can be an effective way to demonstrate to your children that you care about the things they care about.

When asked with an attitude of genuine curiosity rather than judgment (and kids always know the difference), "what" and "how" questions can be an effective way to demonstrate to your children that you care about the things they care about, that you're willing to keep an open mind (at least for a while), and that you're willing to enter their world to better understand them. Here are some examples:

"What do you like about hanging out with that group of kids?"
"How do you think you'd feel if someone said that to you?"
"How does _____ make you feel?"
"What do you think you might want to do differently next time?"

Remember, attitude counts: Your children will know if you're not really interested in what they have to say. You may not like everything you hear, but the more you are able to understand your children's perspective, the better able you will be to guide their behavior and stay close to their hearts.

3. Explore the world of play. Picture a simple scene: Two young boys are walking single file along the top of a rock wall, grinning and holding their arms out for balance. Right behind them (and smiling just as broadly) comes their father. This may not look like an exercise in effective parenting, but it is. One of the best ways to understand children, particularly young ones, is to play with them. And many adults these days have forgotten something very important: how to play.

Play is truly a child's "work." An infant learns about the permanence of people and things by playing "peek-a-boo" with her parents; she learns about her body by being bounced and tickled. As children grow older, play becomes the laboratory in which they explore their world. They develop social skills, acquire manners, and learn the complicated concept of sharing.

Children learn about gravity; they run, jump, and fall down. They try on new roles and personalities by dressing up and playing all the familiar "let's pretend" games: house and army and good-guys-against-the-bad-guys. And all too often, adults merely watch from the outside.

Oh, parents are good at taking children places where *they* can play. You probably drive your children to play group, to child care, to gymnastics or soccer. But you may sometimes find it hard to get involved yourself. Many parents prefer structured activities to unstructured playtime—organized games and groups are easier to plan for in a busy day. But children need unscheduled time to explore the world of imagination. When was the last time you played dress-up with your child? That you got down on the floor and participated in a vigorous

One of the best ways to understand children is to play with them.

game of Legos or Barbie? When did you last play "hide-and-seek" with all the lights turned off? Or have a real water fight, with squirt guns, hoses, and water balloons?

Yes, it's hard to find time. By the end of the day, most parents are weary and longing for nothing more than a quiet moment. The request "Read to me, Mommy," or "Play with me, Daddy," can feel more like a burden than an opportunity.

But there's no real substitute for laughing until your ribs ache. Do you want to get into your child's world, to understand how he thinks and feels, what he dreams about? Then learn to play—*really* play. Get muddy; get rug burns on your knees. Walk along rock walls; go in-line skating. Learn to pretend; let your child teach you his favorite video game (yes, you'll probably lose). If your children are older, consider active play that the entire family can enjoy. A day of skiing, hiking, or bicycling usually leaves everyone feeling closer. And remember to laugh—a lot. Play is good for parents, too.

> It is sad but true that many young people know far more about their favorite recording artists or television celebrities than they do about members of their own family.

4. Be aware of the influence of technology and culture. When lack of connection in a family creates a void, our culture—the media, advertising, television, movies, and music that surround us—will step in to fill it. It is sad but true that many young people know far more about their favorite recording artists or television celebrities than they do about members of their own family.

Technology has become a part of everyday family life. We are surrounded by video recorders, CD players, televisions, computers, and the Internet. All of this technology holds wonderful benefits—but there are dangers, too. Many children and teens spend hours watching television or "surfing the Net" in their rooms, while time for family meetings, conversation, and connection is rare. Television has become the family baby-sitter: in some homes, it is never turned off.

Television in particular poses risks to children. Watching television is an entirely passive activity: it does not teach language and is not as educational as most parents think. Young children especially need a great deal of supervision where TV is concerned because they are unable to differentiate well between reality and fantasy and do not exercise judgment or critical thinking skills while watching. Advertising, too, has a powerful effect on young people, who often have a surprising amount of money of their own to spend these days.

It certainly is not necessary to take your big screen to the dump or to ban your children from the computer or movie theater. But it is wise to be aware of the power that culture wields over young minds. Watch television *with* your children; use "what" and "how" questions to talk with them about what you see and hear. If you have a computer, consider putting it in a shared space in your home; teach your children about Internet safety.

> Stepfamilies require courage and creativity from the people who form them.

Better yet, turn off the electronics from time to time and talk to each other. Did you feel a glitch in your stomach at the very thought of doing such a thing? If so, you may be as addicted to electronics as your children are. (Yes, electronics can be addicting.)

Modern conveniences can be assets, but sometimes they drive wedges between people rather than drawing them together. Lasting connection rarely grows out of a television set.

5. Share your own history. Take a moment sometime soon and ask your child what he or she thinks you do all day long, where you grew up, or what your favorite things were when you were a child. The answers you get may surprise you. Children frequently know very little about their parents and stepparents as *people*.

Part of creating connection with children is being willing to share yourself with them—especially in stepfamilies, in which some of the members may know very little about others. There are many fun and interesting ways to teach your children about yourself. Here are a few suggestions:

• Invite each member of the family to "interview" an extended family member, then present their findings to the rest of the family at a family meeting. One family invited a grandfather to share his experiences, souvenirs, and memories from World War II as part of a child's school assignment. They were all amazed at how connected to each other they felt afterward.

• Get out old scrapbooks and photo albums, and share memories and stories about your own childhood, adolescence, and young adulthood. Don't be afraid of painful memories; they have a surprising potential to draw you closer to those you love. Sometimes it helps children drop their own defenses when they realize their parents are as human—and as susceptible to hurt and longing—as they are.

• Take your child to work with you for a day. Many children love to explore a parent's office or workplace, and it can help them understand when you need time to relax and recharge at the end of a busy day.

• Invite children to join you at concerts and performances that you enjoy, then offer to go with them to their own. Or read aloud to children from the books you loved at their age.

Your own imagination and creativity will give you even more suggestions. Building bridges of understanding between you and your children is always a good idea.

6. Use discipline to teach and guide. We'll explore discipline in detail in later chapters; for the moment, it may surprise you to learn that one of the ways children learn to trust and respect parents (and stepparents) is when adults offer discipline that is consistent, respectful, and both kind *and* firm. In fact, children often test boundaries in an effort to learn whether parents really mean what they say.

> Young children are unable to differentiate well between reality and fantasy and do not exercise judgment or critical thinking skills while watching TV.

Punishment and overcontrol, and the opposite extreme of overindulgence and permissiveness, create distrust, manipulation, and often, resistance. Children have an innate need to know that the adults they depend on can offer strength, security, and structure without harshness or humiliation. Discipline offered with respect and dignity reassures children and goes a long way toward establishing real connection.

7. Be patient. Patience rarely comes easily, especially to stepparents who may feel they don't belong or aren't accepted as a "real parent" in their new family. But trust can never be forced, and hard as it may be, giving children room to feel connection when *they* are ready is usually the wisest course. Spending time, showing curiosity, inviting children to understand you, using discipline to teach and guide, and practicing patience will give you the best opportunity to build lasting relationships with your children and stepchildren.

> Trust can never be forced. Giving children room to feel connection when they are ready is usually the wisest course.

The Importance of Balance

THERE'S NO WAY around it: Effective parenting (and stepparenting) takes a great deal of time—something many adults believe they just don't have enough of. There is so much to cope with in a stepfamily: you must develop emotional health of your own, work toward a strong relationship with your partner, perhaps deal with your ex, and then understand and connect with your children, not to mention earn a living and keep a home running. There is so much to do, and it will undoubtedly feel overwhelming at times.

Stepfamilies require courage and creativity from the people who form them. Remember to take care of yourself and to look for the balance between all the roles and responsibilities you must juggle. Like learning to ride a bicycle, stepfamily life occasionally has its wobbles and crashes; it's all part of the process. Keeping your eyes on your priorities and learning to keep your balance will help you, your partner, and the children you share stay strong and connected.

12

Understanding Behavior

The Mistaken Goals of
Behavior in Your Stepfamily

BEING A PARENT or a stepparent in a stepfamily has two parts. One is the "step" part: all of those issues and situations that result from your life with a new partner and the changes in lifestyle to which your family must adjust. The other is the part we often tend to forget: the good old-fashioned "parent" part. Despite the fact that you are now a stepfamily, some things *haven't* changed. You still need to learn to understand and respond effectively to children's behavior—and misbehavior.

It may be helpful to remember that most of the problems you experience with your children are normal. Because neither adults nor children are perfect, a certain amount of disagreement and rule bending is inevitable. Many newly remarried parents believe that every misbehavior is directly related to their new family situation when that may not be the case at all.

The adjustments inherent in becoming a stepfamily may prove to be a blessing in disguise: They present you with a valuable opportunity to increase your awareness and to learn new parenting skills. Dealing with a new situation can wake us up and signal that we need to make changes. Many parents fall into the habit of reacting to misbehavior without thinking much about it. Such a reaction usually takes the form of punishment, lecturing, shaming, or other actions that are not only ultimately ineffective but that are also often counterproductive over time. Other parents overreact by thinking too much. This extreme often takes the form of guilt, permissiveness, and overprotection of children. Parent education, through books like this one or through parenting classes, helps parents learn to take thoughtful action instead of just reacting (or overreacting). Effective parenting usually proves to be a combination of two equally important factors: lots of good information and the ability to trust your own inner wisdom, common sense, and understanding of your own child.

> Despite the fact that you are now a stepfamily, you still need to understand and respond effectively to children's behavior—and misbehavior.

All parents struggle with their children occasionally, and all children misbehave. The good news is that children's behavior contains clues that a wise adult can learn to read. These clues provide you with valuable information about why your children behave as they do and how you can respond in a way that helps them choose better behavior. Some of what your children are doing is certainly due to adjustments you all must make to be part of a stepfamily, but some behavior occurs just because they're at "that age" or because they have the same needs and feelings that all children do. How can you interpret your children's misbehavior and learn to deal with it effectively—and with love, dignity, and mutual respect?

Getting into Your Child's World

PARENTS OFTEN OVERLOOK one of the most helpful clues to understanding behavior. As we have already learned, when you deal with a person who is younger than you are, you must remember to look at the world through that person's eyes. In the case of small children, those eyes are much closer to the ground and see the world in an entirely different way!

A two-year-old who accidentally spills her milk or forgets her toys out in the yard is not misbehaving; her behavior is developmentally appropriate. Simply put, she's just doing what two-year-olds do! A four-year-old who tells you he saw a tiger behind the bushes isn't lying; he's exercising a lively imagination and sense of creativity. All children are egocentric, which means that they are the center of their own universe. This doesn't mean they are spoiled or self-ish; it does mean they may feel responsible for adult anger or have a perfectly normal desire to be the center of attention and to see everything that happens in relation to themselves. A helpful, loving response to developmentally appropriate behaviors is teaching new skills—and sometimes, entering into the spirit of the moment and having fun! Understanding "developmental appropriateness" does not mean accepting poor behavior, but it does affect the way you approach *changing* that behavior.

> Effective parenting is a combination of two equally important factors: good information and the ability to trust your inner wisdom, common sense, and understanding of your child.

Teenagers, too, are experiencing developmental changes, sometimes known as hormones. Teens want independence from you; they also want connection and acceptance. This would be a tough balance to achieve even without the physical and emotional changes of adolescence; when you throw everything into the mix and add in a stepparent or two for good measure, life can become amazingly complicated for everyone involved.

A wise and loving parent will take a moment to get into his or her child's world and to understand what life looks like through a child's eyes. Children's behavior can be irritating and annoying; they create messes and ask questions

and try our patience on a regular basis. Still, not every annoying thing they do is misbehavior. Learning about your child's unique development and personality and taking the time to connect with him can save both of you a great deal of anguish and misunderstanding.

So What *Is* Misbehavior?

RANDY ARRIVED AT the counselor's office with an agenda. As soon as the greetings were out of the way, he dove right in.

"It's my son, Matthew," he said, when the counselor invited him to speak. "He's 15, and he's turned into a horrible bragger. Every time someone in the family tells about something that's happened to them, Matt can top them. His clothes are cooler, he's a better athlete, he's better at computers—it's starting to get on all of our nerves. And I worry about Matt; no one will want to be around him if he keeps up like this."

"Well, let's begin by finding out more about your family," the counselor said. "Who's in your family, anyway?"

"There's me, and there's Matt. Then there's Martha, my wife. We got married about two years ago," Randy said, putting an arm around the elegant brunette sitting next to him, a baby cradled in her arms. "There's Michael, Martha's son from her first marriage. He's 18 and the starting quarterback for his high school team. He's not here today because he has practice."

The counselor nodded in recognition, and Randy smiled proudly. "He's had a great year—been in all the papers. The college scouts are checking him out, and we expect him to get a good scholarship somewhere. Last but not least, there's Chelsea here. She's our new baby, just two months old."

The counselor looked over at Matthew, who sat slumped in a chair with a baseball cap pulled low over his face. "Looks like you're not too thrilled about being here today, Matt," he said. "Is there anything you can tell me about your family?"

When Matt didn't answer, Randy leaned over and put a hand on his son's knee. "We're here because we want things to be better, kiddo," he said gently. "You're not in trouble, and you can be honest."

Matthew looked doubtful, but he did answer the counselor's question. "I don't mean to brag—I know it's rude to do that, and I know it bugs my dad and stepmother. I guess things just come out wrong."

As Matthew began to tell his story, a picture emerged of a confused teenager, caught between an impossibly cool and popular stepbrother and an adorable new baby girl. Matthew's body wasn't cooperating with him, either; he had a mild case of acne, and his voice still squeaked when he got excited. He was a good student and had a close circle of friends, but somehow nothing he did seemed impressive compared to his siblings' assets and accomplishments. Martha seemed okay, but he didn't really know her very well, and, anyway, she was usually busy with the baby. Matthew finished his story with an eloquent sigh.

"Tell me something," the counselor said, looking at Randy and Martha. "How do you folks feel when Matthew brags?"

Randy considered for a moment, then shrugged. "Irritated, I guess, and annoyed," he said. "He's a good boy, and I love him. I just get frustrated when he interrupts everyone to boast about something he has or something he's done."

"I feel worried," Martha said, with a smile at Matt. "And I guess I feel a bit guilty. I haven't had much time to spend with Matt, what with all of Michael's games and with Chelsea here to take care of. I'm an older mom, as you can see," she laughed, "and pregnancy was a bit tough this time around. I've probably been pretty preoccupied."

The counselor looked around the circle and smiled. "You folks deserve a lot of credit. You care about each other, and you want to make things better—that's an excellent beginning. As you've probably discovered, starting a stepfamily can be a challenge.

"The feelings you have about Matt's bragging give me clues to what's going on for him," the counselor continued. "My guess is that without really planning it or meaning to, Matt has discovered a behavior that gets him some attention. If you look at life in your family from his perspective, it's not too hard to understand why he might feel like he needs attention. A football star and a baby are tough competition, aren't they, Matt?"

Matthew nodded glumly.

> When children fail to feel a sense of belonging, they become discouraged and may choose what Rudolf Dreikurs called a "mistaken goal of behavior."

"What can we do to help?" Randy asked. "We don't want Matt to have to compete for our attention—we love him for who he is. Do you have any suggestions?"

Breaking the Code

As their counselor would explain to Martha and Randy, children need to find a sense of belonging and significance. They need to know they have worth and are accepted just for who they are. When children fail to feel a sense of belonging, they become discouraged and may choose what Rudolf Dreikurs, author of *Children: The Challenge,* called a "mistaken goal of behavior." We call them "mistaken goals" because a child mistakenly believes the behavior will help him regain a sense of belonging.

It's true that a misbehaving child simply wants to belong and is sending us that message in a sort of "code." Perhaps the most important part of dealing with a child's misbehavior is remembering that there is *always* a belief behind the behavior (although children are usually unaware on a conscious level of what that belief is). You will be a more effective parent when you can learn to change a child's perception of his world—his beliefs about himself and others—rather than just trying to change the behavior itself.

Four common mistaken goals—undue attention, power, revenge, and assumed inadequacy—are presented in detail in the Mistaken Goal Chart (p. 172). We have already discovered that children in stepfamilies sometimes feel dethroned, displaced, or upstaged. How do these mistaken goals look in your family, and how do you decipher which one you're seeing?

Three clues will help you understand your child's mistaken goal of behavior:

1. Your feelings. Randy and Martha felt irritated, annoyed, worried, and guilty about Matthew's behavior—good clues that his mistaken goal was undue attention. When you want to understand your children's behavior, the first thing to check is how *you* feel. When it is power a child is after, adults will feel challenged, threatened, or provoked. The mistaken goal of revenge often triggers feelings of hurt, disappointment, or disgust, while assumed inadequacy usually prompts adults to feel hopeless and helpless. The Mistaken Goal Chart will show you how to use your feelings to decipher a child's mistaken goal.

2. Your reactions. Adults often respond to the behavior of each mistaken goal in predictable ways, almost like a dance in which each person knows the steps. When Matthew would brag about how much cooler he was than

"BREAKING THE CODE" OF BEHAVIOR

Parents can "break the code" of a child's behavior by looking at three clues:

1. Your feelings

2. Your reactions

3. The child's response

Mistaken Goal Chart

The child's goal is:	If the parent/stepparent feels:	And tends to react by:	And if the child's response is:	The belief behind the child's behavior is:	Coded messages:	Parent/stepparent proactive and empowering responses include:
Undue attention (to keep others busy or to get special service)	Annoyed Irritated Worried Guilty	Reminding Coaxing Doing things for the child he/she could do for him/herself	Stops temporarily, but later assumes same or another disturbing behavior	I count (belong) only when I'm being noticed or getting special service. I'm only important when I'm keeping you busy with me.	Notice me. Involve me usefully.	"I love you and _____." (Example: I care about you and will spend time with you later."); redirect by assigning a task so child can gain useful attention; avoid special service; plan special time; set up routines; use problem-solving; encourage; use family meetings; touch without words; ignore; set up nonverbal signals.
Misguided power (to be boss)	Angry Challenged Threatened Defeated	Fighting Giving in Thinking "You can't get away with it" or "I'll make you" Wanting to be right	Intensifies behavior Defiant compliance Feels he/she's won when parent/teacher is upset Passive power	I belong only when I'm boss, in control, or proving no one can boss me. "You can't make me."	Let me help. Give me choices.	Redirect to positive power by asking for help; offer limited choices; don't fight and don't give in; withdraw from conflict; be firm and kind; act, don't talk; decide what you will do; let routines be the boss; leave and calm down; develop mutual respect; set a few reasonable limits; practice follow-through; encourage; use family meetings.
Revenge (to get even)	Hurt Disappointed Disbelieving Disgusted	Retaliating Getting even Thinking "How could you do this to me?"	Retaliates Intensifies Escalates the same behavior or chooses another weapon	I don't think I belong so I'll hurt others as I feel hurt. I can't be liked or loved.	I'm hurting; validate my feelings.	Acknowledge hurt feelings; avoid feeling hurt; avoid punishment and retaliation; build trust; use active listening; share your feelings; make amends; show you care; act, don't talk; encourage strengths; put kids in same boat; use family meetings.
Assumed inadequacy (to give up and be left alone)	Despair Hopeless Helpless Inadequate	Giving up Doing for Overhelping	Retreats further Passive No improvement No response	I can't belong because I'm not perfect, so I'll convince others not to expect anything of me; I am helpless and unable; it's no use trying because I won't do it right.	Don't give up on me. Show me a small step.	Break task down to small steps; stop all criticism; encourage any positive attempt; have faith in child's abilities; focus on assets; don't pity; don't give up; set up opportunities for success; teach skills; show how, but don't do for; enjoy the child; build on his/her interests; encourage, encourage, encourage; use family meetings.

Michael or a friend, his father would lecture him or nag him about how unpleasant his boasting was. Matthew would stop for a while but would usually resume his behavior later. The Mistaken Goal Chart will show you some typical adult reactions to children's behavior for each goal.

3. The child's response. As we have seen, Matthew's bragging and boasting didn't stop, no matter how often his father and stepmother mentioned it. The chart will show you some of the ways children typically respond when adults react to their misbehavior.

Remember, the Mistaken Goal Chart is a tool to help you understand your child's misbehavior. It is less important to figure out *the* goal than it is to understand that there is a belief behind the behavior and to work to change a child's mistaken beliefs about himself, others, and his world. Getting into the child's world often requires guessing. The clues we have discussed make it easier to guess, but you still may be wrong. Guessing is not about being right or wrong; it is about gaining understanding. If you guess incorrectly, your child will let you know. If you are right, your child will feel understood. So, make a guess and check it out with your child. You might say, "Could it be that you are feeling upset about _____?" or "I'll bet that really hurt your feelings." (Remember your communication skills!) Sometimes an apology is required: "I'm sorry that I overreacted. I was afraid for you, but you may have thought I didn't care about you." Use your wisdom and listen to your heart when making guesses, and you will know what to say. When children feel understood, they are more likely to be open to solutions.

Seeking Solutions

WHEN MATTHEW AND his family returned to the counselor's office, things had changed a bit. Randy and Martha had begun to understand how Matt's world felt to him and that his need for their attention was genuine and important. They recognized that Matthew was right about some things: Michael's football career and Chelsea's birth had distracted them, and Matthew felt displaced and less important. When they understood the belief behind his bragging, dealing with it became easier.

Martha and Randy decided to help Matthew get attention in positive ways. They found many suggestions for positive interaction in the last column of the Mistaken Goal Chart. Martha began showing an interest in Matt's activities, taking a few moments each day to ask him "what" and "how" questions about his day, his friends, and his schoolwork. She invited his help with the baby and began taking Chelsea to Matt's soccer games. The guys on the team thought Chelsea was "cool," and Matt glowed as they gathered around to tickle and admire his baby sister.

Randy began scheduling "special time" with Matthew, even taking him along to work occasionally. Even Michael helped, inviting Matthew to hang out with his friends once or twice and asking Matthew's opinion on which college offer he should accept. While Matthew's bragging did not disappear overnight, he became a more cheerful, confident young man. When he slipped back into his boastful ways, Randy and Martha chose to ignore it rather than to lecture and nag. Slowly, the family grew together and became more able to recognize the special abilities and qualities of every member.

It is important to note that different children develop different beliefs in similar situations. For example, Matthew chose the mistaken goal of undue attention. Another child in a similar situation might choose the mistaken goal of power and decide to rebel. This child might decide to stay out late or refuse to cooperate in numerous ways. Another child might feel hurt or rejected and choose the mistaken goal of revenge. This child might say or do hurtful things to get even. Often a revengeful child hurts herself as much as others by doing such things as refusing to succeed in school. Another child might choose the mistaken goal of assumed inadequacy and simply withdraw, disappearing from family life in a cloud of discouragement.

> Different children develop different beliefs in similar situations.

When dealing with misbehavior, it is usually most helpful to focus on understanding and finding solutions. The Mistaken Goal Chart's last column focuses on positive and encouraging ways to deal with the belief behind a child's behavior. The next chapter will provide some useful tools for finding solutions for your family.

The first step, though, is always understanding. Make an effort to get into your child's world. Consider his developmental stage and his personality. Look at the world as your child perceives it, and check your own feelings and responses. Break the code, and see if you can discover your child's mistaken goal. If you can, you will be well on your way to handling misbehavior in a way that builds trust, understanding, and respect.

13

Discipline in Your Stepfamily

NOT TOO MANY years ago, you might have heard a parent tell a child (perhaps not entirely in jest), "If you don't behave yourself, I'm going to beat you like a stepchild!" Remember the "wicked stepmother" and the "cruel stepfather"? They often acquired their nasty reputations from the way they dealt with misbehavior and handed out punishment—everything from whippings to floor scrubbings. And the stepchild was usually the one who suffered.

We like to think that we are more enlightened these days. We know that beatings aren't the answer, and most of us would never intentionally treat a stepchild more harshly than a birth child. But the simple truth is that most parents still grapple with the idea of discipline. What is it? How are we supposed to do it? Is it wrong to give a kid a swat now and then? Is it possible to treat children with love and respect and still maintain order and boundaries?

Children need discipline; they long for it. Discipline, however, is not the same thing as punishment. Loving, consistent discipline is one of the best ways to create trust and security in a family. Still, because no other issue causes as much disagreement and stress in stepfamilies as does discipline, it is important to decide who is responsible for discipline and how it will be handled. Children—especially stepchildren—may perceive a lack of interest in their behavior (and unwillingness to discipline) as a lack of caring. On the other hand, overcontrol is threatening and may result in resistance and rebellion. How, then, can parents—and stepparents—practice discipline that helps create the responsible, respectful, resourceful people we want our children to become?

> Loving, consistent discipline is one of the best ways to create trust and security in a family.

"We've Tried Everything . . ."

Q: I am a mother who is involved in a nasty, ongoing custody dispute with my ex-husband. My current husband is more of a father than my daughter has ever had before. We encounter constant conflict from my ex over the issue of discipline.

It is very difficult for the birth parent always to be the disciplinarian. My eight-year-old daughter has lived with us for a year and just received her first spanking from her stepfather. We had tried everything, and since the spanking, the misbehavior has stopped. In fact, their relationship has deepened because she now views him as an equal parent in our home. We felt this was necessary because we have a son together and want consistent discipline for both our children.

I want to know whether you agree with spanking and whether there are laws about stepparents spanking their stepchildren. My ex has threatened to sue for custody because of the spanking; he never disciplines my daughter in any way and hasn't since the divorce. Don't we have the right to discipline our daughter in our own home?

A: Your question raises a number of interesting issues. First, the question about whether a stepparent is allowed to discipline a child is a legal one and depends entirely on how the "discipline" is conducted. In many states, anything that leaves a physical mark, such as a bruise or handprint, is considered abuse and can be prosecuted. It certainly would provide fuel for a custody fight.

More important, perhaps, is the idea of what "discipline" actually is. When they say they have "tried everything," most parents mean they have tried every punishment they can think of—grounding, shaming, taking away privileges, lecturing, and so on. Punishment seems to work for the moment, but you can't be sure what your daughter is really thinking, feeling—or deciding to do in the future. True discipline teaches life skills and focuses on solutions. It's entirely possible that by understanding your daughter's mistaken goal of behavior, helping her feel belonging in your home, and building respectful relationships among her, you, and your husband, the behavior would have stopped without the spanking.

The Art of Effective Discipline

IT'S IMPORTANT FOR all parents and stepparents to look at exactly what discipline is. As it turns out, when people talk about *discipline,* they usually mean *punishment.* In reality, the two concepts are not at all the same. *Discipline* comes from the Latin root *disciplina*—the same root from which we get the word *disciple,* which means "one who follows truth, principle, or a venerated leader." *Discipline* also means "to teach or to educate." *Education* comes from the root word *educare,* which means "to draw forth." Parents are not teaching or educating when they scold, lecture, use too much control, or punish. All these methods are designed to "stuff in" instead of to "draw forth."

> When people talk about *discipline,* they usually mean *punishment.* In reality, the two concepts are not at all the same.

In other words, discipline that is effective develops self-discipline from within the child by helping the child figure out what causes problems and how to solve them. Punishment reinforces an external sense of control; a child expects punishment or rewards from others in response to his or her behavior. Think about it: When discipline involves punishment and rewards, who is responsible? The adult is responsible for "catching" children being "good" so that rewards can be offered, and for "catching" children being "bad" so punishment can be doled out. What happens when the adult is not around? Effective discipline means using methods that help children learn the self-discipline and responsibility required to develop important life skills, such as cooperation, respect, concern for self and others, and problem solving.

Do these definitions turn your ideas about discipline upside down? If so, this is a good place to start. Perhaps, instead of fighting about old ways of disciplining, the parents in a new stepfamily can start over and learn together how to discipline effectively.

This can be revolutionary for stepfamilies in which a great deal of discord stems from arguments about who should discipline the children, the "real" parent or the stepparent. When punishment is eliminated, discord and arguments are eliminated. Punishment is negative and is especially difficult to watch when it is done by "someone else." Even in non-stepfamilies, a father may not like the way the mother "disciplines." However, he can't use the excuse, "I don't want you to spank *my* child."

> Effective discipline means using methods that develop important life skills such as cooperation, respect, concern for self and others, and problem solving.

Discipline, on the other hand, is positive and can be a pleasure to experience or to watch. "Real" parents can hardly object when they see a stepparent gently helping a child explore what happened, what caused it to happen, what the child learned from it, how she can use what she learned in the future, and what she can do now to solve the problem. This is just one example of Positive Discipline that is nonpunitive. More ideas will be discussed later.

Most of us have absorbed our ideas about discipline from our own parents, our experiences, our society, and years of tradition. All parents occasionally disagree about the best way to provide discipline, but in stepfamilies, in which each partner may have different experiences and beliefs about what discipline is and how it ought to be done, those disagreements can feel especially intense. Often the children are caught in the middle. Now is the time for both parents to leave old ideas of punishment behind them.

The Problem with Punishment

AS WE'VE ALREADY learned, children are constantly making decisions about life, themselves, and what they need to do to belong. Children who experience discipline designed to teach usually learn to weigh the consequences of their actions and behave accordingly. (Well, most of the time, anyway!) On the other hand, children who experience punishment may not be making the decisions adults think they are.

For instance, many parents are fond of telling misbehaving children, "Go to your room and think about what you did!" We have to wonder whether parents think this through. Do they believe they can control their children's thoughts? Do parents believe their children obediently think about what they did? Or do most children go to their rooms and think about what their *parents* did—how unfair, mean, and ridiculous they are?

Many people still believe that children won't learn to behave unless they are made to suffer at least a little. And the seductive thing about punishment—such things as grounding, spanking, taking away privileges, and shaming—is that it seems to work, at least for the moment. But sometimes we need to beware of what works. Studies have shown that over time punishment creates young people who actually misbehave more often and who have fewer problem-solving skills, less self-confidence, and fewer successful relationships with others.

Punishment often teaches children unintended lessons: to misbehave when the enforcers aren't around, to get even if possible, to become sneaky or rebellious, or to focus on the "mean old parent" (or the "wicked stepmother") rather than on the behavior that got them into trouble in the first place.

Loving Discipline in Your Stepfamily

THE BEST KIND of discipline is proactive, and many of the skills and ideas we've already explored in previous chapters will help you avoid a great deal of

KEYS TO POSITIVE DISCIPLINE IN YOUR STEPFAMILY

Here are suggestions to consider when deciding what discipline will look like in your family:

1. Explore with your partner your approach to discipline.
2. Work toward consistency.
3. Focus on solutions.
4. Foster cooperation, not competition.
5. Be aware of your children's development, abilities, and limitations.
6. Take one step at a time.
7. Remember that children do what "works."
8. See mistakes—including your own—as opportunities to learn.
9. Be kind *and* firm.
10. If your child travels between homes, recognize that each is autonomous.

misbehavior. When misbehavior happens (and sooner or later, it always does), how can you respond in ways that help children choose better behavior next time as well as to believe in their ability to succeed? How do partners who are combining families, philosophies, and children practice loving, effective discipline?

It should be said that nothing works all the time for all children and all adults; after all, no one is perfect. There is simply no substitute for patience, good communication skills, and understanding the beliefs behind children's behavior. Here are some ideas you might consider when deciding what form discipline will take in your family:

1. Explore with your partner your approach to discipline. Think discipline through—and the sooner, the better! If you're reading this book before marrying again, there is no better time than the present for exploring how you will approach discipline. If you've already joined your families and begun dealing with discipline, it's never too late. Hold a couple's meeting sometime soon, and put discipline on the agenda. Explore what each of you learned about discipline in your original families, how you handled it in the past, and what you might like to do differently. What has worked well to reduce misbehavior? What has not? What are each of you comfortable with? When exploring these issues, be sure to think through the long-range results of what you are doing. In other words, has your discipline worked to stop misbehavior but created low self-esteem or rebellion? Has your discipline stopped misbehavior and helped your children learn important life skills and self-confidence? Or has it failed to stop misbehavior at all?

If discipline is indeed about helping children to make better choices, how can you and your partner work together to accomplish that goal? Consider the ideas and methods in this book and see what "fits" for you and your children. Listen to your own wisdom and knowledge of your children, and decide to try the things you both believe will give you the best result.

2. Work toward consistency. No one is consistent all of the time, but as much as possible, try to be sure that the rules you have are few, firm, and fair. Are the rules the same for all of the children— resident and visiting, stepchildren and birth children? Are children learning to respect both adults in the family, stepparent and birth parent? (Children learn respect when they live with adults who respect others.) As much as possible, rules and boundaries in a stepfamily should apply to everyone's children, and all children and adults should be treated with respect. As soon as the children are old enough, be sure they are included in creating

> It should be said that nothing works all the time for all children and all adults; after all, no one is perfect.

rules. Respectfully involving children in the creation of rules is one way to educate by "drawing forth" their ideas and their commitment. Remember, family meetings are an excellent way to accomplish this goal.

3. Focus on solutions. The importance of keeping your focus on solutions (rather than blame) can't be overemphasized. The urge to punish is deeply ingrained in us and in our culture, but learning happens (and you will usually get better results) when you focus on finding solutions to problems rather than handing out punishment. Punishment deals only with the past and is designed to make children pay for what they have done. Solutions focus on the future and help children change their behavior the next time they encounter a similar situation. Sometimes talking together, exploring feelings, actions, and results to identify what could be done differently next time, is enough. If the situation requires action, think things through in advance: What will your children *really* learn? What will they think, feel, and decide about themselves—and about you? Again, involve your children.

Too many parents "tell" children what happened, what caused it to happen, how they should feel about it, and what they should do about it—classic "stuffing in." The best discipline takes place when children are encouraged to explore for themselves what happened, what caused it to happen, what they learned from the experience, and what they will do in the future using their experience as a basis when they brainstorm for solutions—"drawing forth." Yes, this takes more time. Learning, development, and real growth usually do.

> Rules and boundaries in a stepfamily should apply to everyone's children, and all children and adults should be treated with respect.

4. Foster cooperation, not competition. Let all members of the family know that you value cooperation—working together to solve a problem. Begin by valuing everyone's feelings and welcoming new ideas and suggestions (a family meeting is a good place to start). Let yourself be a learner; your partner (or your child) might have a better way to handle a situation. Stepfamilies truly become families when they work together.

5. Be aware of your children's development, abilities, and limitations. Discipline is very different for toddlers than for children who have reached the age of reason (around four years old). Before the age of reason, parents need to provide more structure and apply it with kindness and firmness. Kindness shows respect for the child; firmness shows respect for what needs to be done.

Young children need supervision, and distraction is the most effective discipline tool. In other words, a two-year-old is not developmentally ready to understand danger. Parents must protect them from danger—not by spanking "to teach" them something they are not able to learn but by distracting them. Distraction means to kindly and firmly remove them from what they can't do (put a fork in the electrical socket) and lead them to what they can do (play with the plastic lids). Remember, you probably will have to repeat even the most effective Positive Discipline tools more than once or twice: Children usually learn best through patient teaching and repetition. Another important discipline tool for this age is to decide what *you* will do instead of what you will try to make your *child* do. For example, keep forks out of reach, cover exposed sockets, and kindly and firmly remove the child from danger.

As children get older, taking time for training is an excellent discipline tool. For example, take your three-year-old for a walk. When you approach an intersection, ask your child to look up and then down the street and tell you if cars are coming. Obviously three-, four-, and five-year-olds still need supervision, but taking time for training teaches them by drawing forth information so they will have inner wisdom by the time they are old enough to walk to the park by themselves.

You can start getting children involved in the problem-solving process around the age of four. At this age, children have excellent ideas for solving problems when provided the opportunity to voice their opinions. There are many more effective discipline tools, as you will see in the next chapter. Our point here is to emphasize the importance of considering developmental appropriateness and personality differences.

Remember that each child is unique. Your partner's child may find it easy to sit quietly in a restaurant. If your child does not, go prepared with books, crayons, and small toys. Parent the child you have rather than expecting that child to change. Planning ahead and being prepared are among the best discipline tools.

6. Take one step at a time. Especially when your family is new, choose to focus your attention on the things that matter. Almost everything related to children can become a battle if we let it. Talk with your partner and decide which issues must be dealt with kindly and firmly and which issues you can afford to handle more flexibly. Would you rather focus on chores or homework? Church attendance or hairstyle? When you have decided what matters most, communicate clearly, do lots of teaching (in the true sense of the word), get older children involved in brainstorming for solutions, and follow through with dignity and respect.

7. Remember that children do what "works." If a child learns that throwing a tantrum, being disrespectful to his stepdad, or threatening to go live with Mom gets a reactive response, he will almost certainly do it again. How do you respond to your child's actions? Does his behavior "work" for him? Are you reacting, or thoughtfully responding with Positive Discipline?

> Parent the child you have rather than expecting that child to change.

Understanding the four mistaken goals of behavior (discussed in chapter 12) can help you avoid getting hooked by manipulative behavior. Instead of reacting to the mistaken goal, you can respond in encouraging ways that meet your child's deeper needs to belong and to feel significant.

8. See mistakes—including your own—as opportunities to learn. No matter how much good information you have and no matter how good your intentions, most parents occasionally get hooked into reacting to irritating behavior. That's okay. Your mistakes will give you and your family the opportunity to learn about apologies, forgiveness, and making up. Sometimes, when you focus on solutions and on creating trust and acceptance, things can actually be better after a mistake.

Have you ever noticed how forgiving children can become when you apologize? An apology usually changes the relationship energy and creates an atmosphere that is conducive to problem solving. And you have just modeled the importance of taking personal responsibility and apologizing. You have also helped your child learn that mistakes are the beginning, not the end. When children don't learn to see mistakes as opportunities for learning, they often see mistakes as evidence of their inadequacy or as failure. Either conclusion is discouraging.

9. Be kind *and* firm. As we mentioned earlier, kindness shows respect for the child (and yourself); firmness shows respect for what needs to be done. Yes, you can be both at the same time—in fact, it's usually the most effective way to deal with young people. You can smile, accept and validate children's feelings, and use a friendly tone of voice—and still follow through with dignity and respect. Effective discipline does not mean yelling, frowning, or being unpleasant. Because being firm and kind does take self-control and practice, be sure you are able to handle your own emotions in a healthy manner.

Being kind and firm at the same time is one of the most effective tools you can learn. Sometimes what could have been effective discipline turns into punishment because a parent forgets to be kind as well as firm. Conversely, discipline sometimes turns into permissiveness because a parent forgets to be firm as well as kind. If you have a problem being kind and firm at the same time, you might try exploring why you have difficulty with either one. Are you too kind because you fear rejection as a result of firmness? Are you too firm because you fear kindness looks weak? Are you reacting instead of being proactive? These are just a few of the many possibilities. Whatever the problem, we promise that you will experience more effective discipline by being kind and firm at the same time than from any other discipline tool you can use.

> Sometimes, when you focus on solutions and on creating trust and acceptance, things can actually be better after a mistake.

10. If your child travels between homes, recognize that each is autonomous. It is neither wise nor helpful to expect your ex to carry out your discipline decisions or to use time with your child's other parent as a punishment or reward. It is undoubtedly frustrating when your child's other home

does not practice discipline in the same way you do, but your child can adapt to the differences between her homes and should be allowed to have an open, respectful relationship with all of the adults in her life. Be assured that practicing mutual respect and Positive Discipline in your own home truly is enough.

Offering your children loving, respectful, and effective discipline will create a feeling of security, trust, and consistency—qualities that go a long way toward making your new family feel like "home" to all of its members.

14

Putting Positive Discipline to Work

A PERSISTENT MYTH ABOUT stepfamily life is that it should somehow "make up" for the losses and hurts children have experienced. And children in stepfamilies often have experienced quite a lot that is unpleasant. You may feel sorry for your children because they have lost their original family, because they don't like their stepparent, or because they have to share rooms and parental attention. All too often, parents think that letting children off the hook, bending the rules, or giving them special service will somehow make their children's lives easier.

Permissiveness is no more effective than punishment for teaching your children about courage, confidence, and other important life skills. Permissiveness is a mistake many parents make "in the name of love." However, children who are raised permissively grow up thinking others should cater to them instead of learning self-reliance and concern for others.

Guilt can be a useful emotion when it motivates us to examine our lives and consider positive changes. But guilt can also immobilize us or lead us to behave in ways that don't help us—or our children—in the long run. When we let guilt dictate how we handle discipline, we don't do our children any favors.

Marcy and her stepdad don't get along. They have never been close, and lately things seem to be getting worse. Marcy's mom feels bad that the man she married doesn't like her daughter, so she gives Marcy special privileges, buys

her anything she wants, and fails to enforce the few rules she does make. Is it any wonder that Marcy's behavior is deteriorating?

Derek is 14. When his dad married Nancy, Derek wasn't happy; he wanted his own mom to come back. Nancy felt like an intruder (she was partially responsible for the end of the marriage, after all) and compensated by doing everything for Derek, waiting on him, running errands for him, and cooking separate meals when he didn't like what she prepared for his dad. But Derek only became more sullen and demanding. Now he is stealing money from Nancy's purse. What is she to do?

> Permissiveness is no more effective than punishment for teaching your children about courage, confidence, and other important life skills.

In this world of ours where divorce is rampant, many parents work hard outside the home, and life often feels out of balance, there seem to be dozens of reasons to feel guilty about the relationships you have (or may not have) with your children. We'll say it again: Guilt often tempts parents to overcompensate by buying presents, providing lavish activities, or offering special service, but guilt never leads to healthy parenting decisions. If you find that you often feel guilty about your children, let your guilt teach you about the ways you might need to change your priorities. Permissiveness does not help children feel belonging, strange as that may seem.

Children need to know that adults can provide safety and security, and one way they learn this is when adults respond to challenging behavior kindly and firmly. Most parents wonder whether their children and stepchildren will ever learn how to live independent, responsible lives. Effective parenting means being willing to set boundaries, to teach, and to look for solutions to problems even when it might be easier (and feel better) to give in or to provide special service.

Discipline Tools for Stepfamilies

ALMOST ANYTHING CAN be effective discipline when it is done with respect and a genuine desire to teach—and almost anything can be punishment if the desire is to shame or humiliate. Your attitude is the key; children invariably know the difference between a parent's respectful or punishing attitude. The following suggestions are just that—suggestions. You may need to try a variety of methods since nothing works all the time, and you may be comfortable with one idea and uncomfortable with another. Remember to consider mistaken goals; the responses listed on the Mistaken Goal Chart (page 172) may come in handy. Or your own sense of creativity and knowledge of the children in your family may lead you to adapt a suggestion in a way that works for you. Remember to focus on solutions and on teaching, and you'll undoubtedly do just fine.

> One way children know that adults can provide safety and security is when adults respond to challenging behavior kindly and firmly.

Positive Time-Out

WE HAVE LEARNED about positive time-out as a way to help children soothe themselves and manage strong feelings; not surprisingly, it is an effective discipline tool as well, although not when used as a confinement or punishment.

It was the end of a busy afternoon and Margo had absolutely had it. "That's it!" she yelled at seven-year-old Jeanine. "You're in time-out!"

Margo half-pushed, half-dragged her screaming daughter to her room, slamming the door behind her. "Stay in there and think about your attitude until I tell you that you can come out," she said to the closed door.

As she walked away, she heard the ominous sound of toys and books being thrown against the wall—newly painted after their last big argument.

Margo shook her head in frustration. There had to be a better way.

Actually, there is. Time-out is a useful tool in helping children control their behavior—when it's used in an encouraging rather than a punishing way. All of us need to learn self-control, and many people (big and little) handle stress and anger best when they have a moment to cool off and regain their perspective. Remember, we usually do better when we feel better. Helping children handle their stronger emotions can give them skills that will serve them well throughout their lives.

Let's replay the scene between Margo and Jeanine using positive time-out. This mother and daughter have had arguments before, and not long ago they worked together to create a "cool-off" spot in Jeanine's room. In a quiet corner they piled soft pillows and a few familiar stuffed animals. Then they added Jeanine's favorite story tapes, a book or two, and a puzzle.

> When used as encouragement rather than punishment, time-out is a useful tool in helping children control their behavior.

This time, when Jeanine refused to do what her mother asked and became disrespectful, Margo responded by asking her whether she would find it helpful to spend some time in her special spot. "When you feel better, come out and we'll work on a solution to this problem together," she said.

Children rarely refuse to go to a time-out that is set up in this way and sometimes stay there happily for quite a while. Notice that the agreement is that they can come back when they feel better. When children feel better, they automatically do better—or they are at least in a mood for problem solving.

If Jeanine did refuse the suggestion to go to her special place (she might be too upset to be rational), Mom could offer, "Would you like me to go with you?" That offer just might break down Jeanine's defensiveness and invite her cooperation. However, if Jeanine still refuses, Mom could say, "Okay, I think I'll borrow your special place for a while. I need some time to calm down until I feel better."

Mom may need some positive time-out just as much as (or more than) Jeanine does. Even if Mom doesn't, she is still modeling a valuable life skill.

Remember, younger children may do best with a time-out spot in a corner of the room with the rest of the family; older children or teens may prefer an activity to cool off, such as shooting baskets or going outside for a while. When parent and child have agreed on a time-out approach in advance, and it helps a child calm down and get along with others, time-outs can be encouraging instead of punitive.

> When children feel better, they automatically do better—or they are at least in a mood for problem solving.

Parents often object that having a comfortable time-out place rewards children for misbehavior. However, all of us have moments when we just can't seem to get along—and time-out works just as well for adults as it does for children. Letting conflict escalate into a knockdown, drag-out fight rarely does anyone any good. We invite you to see for yourself. (For more information on positive time-out and other ways to avoid power struggles, see *Positive Time Out and Over 50 Ways to Avoid Power Struggles in Homes and Classrooms* [Jane Nelsen, Prima, 1999].)

Here is one final tip about positive time-out: Never let it be your only discipline tool. Some of the following suggestions might be more effective for Jeanine (or your own child) than positive time-out.

Consequences

CONSEQUENCES TEACH CHILDREN BY allowing them to experience the results of their choices. Natural consequences are those things that happen without adult intervention. If you don't eat, for example, you'll probably get hungry. If you don't go to bed early enough, you'll be tired the next morning. Children can learn from these experiences if parents can resist the temptation to lecture, nag, and say, "I told you so!" The best way to deal with natural consequences is to show empathy for what the child is experiencing. Another possibility is to help the child explore what happened, why it happened, and what she learned from the experience—with a sincere interest in the child's point of view.

Remember that exploration takes place when the child is invited to figure things out for herself. Timing is important. Children usually are not in the mood to explore the consequences of their choices when they are upset. Exploration may be an excellent way to *follow up* after some positive time-out.

> Consequences teach children by allowing them to experience the results of their choices.

When there is no natural consequence, however, parents may intervene with a logical consequence. Adults often get hung up in trying to determine "the" consequence for a misbehavior. Consequences can easily become punishments, too, if our aim is to shame and humiliate rather than to teach and find solutions. The best consequences are those in which children have a hand in the design and that focus on preventing future problems.

Consequences should be discussed in advance so that children can make educated choices about their behavior. This sometimes means that children get one "free." For instance, the first time a child fails to put her dirty clothes in the laundry hamper, a parent may choose to pick them up for her and wash them. Then, however, it's time to talk it through. The parent and child may decide together that in the future, clothes that aren't in the hamper won't be

washed. A child who discovers she has no clean clothes to wear to school may decide that picking up is a good idea, and parents can cooperate by offering encouragement and understanding—and by following through without lecturing or nagging. In fact, lectures and nagging will turn what could be a logical consequence into punishment.

Consequences work best with children who are old enough to think logically and understand the connection between their behavior and the consequence. Remember the importance of the child's development; logical reasoning does not develop as soon as most parents think. Take time to communicate: Be sure your child understands what has happened, why you feel the way you do, and what will happen if the behavior is repeated. Be sure you provide a time to try again when the child is ready.

Consequences should always be reasonable, respectful, and related to the misbehavior. For instance, if a child fails to pick up his toys after you've discussed the problem, taking away television privileges is not related; throwing all the toys away is not reasonable. An appropriate consequence might be to put the toys that were not picked up in a trunk or closet for a week and then give the child a chance to try again after exploring what happened last time, what caused it to happen, and what the result of doing that again might be.

> Consequences should always be reasonable, respectful, and related to the misbehavior.

Many parents try to disguise punishment by calling it a logical consequence. Two clues let you know this is occurring: (1) You feel the need to be in control, and (2) a power struggle ensues. You will notice that the consequences described earlier avoid these problems because each has these essential ingredients—the parent deciding what he will do (instead of what he will make the child do), and then following through with kindness, firmness, dignity, and respect.

> Follow-through means that adults decide what *they* will do, then follow through with kind and firm action.

Follow-Through

FOLLOW-THROUGH MEANS that adults decide what *they* will do and then follow through with kind and firm action. As Rudolf Dreikurs has said, to follow through means you "shut your mouth and act." Car behavior provides an excellent example.

The Jones family is excited. They have just finished planning a day at the beach. Seven-year-old Jonathan and five-year-old Jenny have promised that they won't fight. Ken, their stepfather, has warned, "If you do, we'll turn around and come back."

"We won't, we won't!" promise Jonathan and Jenny again.

The Jones family has not gone two miles when a loud wail is heard from the back seat. "Jonathan hit me!"

Jean, the children's mother, says, "What did we tell you kids about fighting?"

Jonathan defends himself, "Well, she touched me."

Ken threatens, "You two had better cut it out, or we are going home."

The children cry out in unison, "Noooooo! We'll be good."

And they are—for about ten minutes. Then another wail is heard. "He took my red crayon!"

Jonathan shouts, "Well, she was hogging it. It's my turn."

Ken—more exasperated now—says, "Do you want me to turn around and go home?"

"Nooooooo. We'll be good."

And so the story goes. Throughout the day Jonathan and Jenny fight, and Ken and Jean make threats. At the end of the day, the adults are tired and angry and threaten never to take the kids anywhere again. Jonathan and Jenny feel bad that they have made their parents so miserable and are beginning to believe they really are bad kids.

Now we'll visit the Smith family. They have just planned their trip to the zoo during their weekly family meeting. Part of the planning included a discussion about limits and consequences. Ross and Diane Smith have told Susan and Sam how miserable they feel when the kids fight. Susan and Sam promise they won't.

Ross said, "I appreciate that, and I think we should come up with a plan for what will happen if you forget." The kids keep insisting they won't fight.

Diane then says, "Well then, is it okay with you if we stop the car if you do forget? We don't think it's safe to drive when you two are fighting, so we'll just pull over to the side of the road and wait for you to stop. You can let us know when you are ready for us to drive again. How do you feel about that solution?" Both kids agree with innocent enthusiasm.

Typically, it doesn't take them long to forget their promise and begin fighting. Diane quickly and quietly pulls off to the side of the road. She and Ross take out magazines and start reading. Each child starts blaming the other while whining about his or her own innocence. Ross and Diane ignore them and just keep reading. It does not take long for Susan to catch on that Mom and Dad must mean what they said.

Susan says, "Okay, we're ready to keep driving."

Ross says, "We'll wait until we hear it from both of you."

Sam, however, is not ready to give in. He pouts, "But she hit me!"

Ross and Diane just keep reading. Susan hits Sam again. "Tell them you're ready," she suggests helpfully.

Sam cries, "She hit me again!" Ross and Diane just keep reading.

Susan realizes that hitting Sam will not help, so she tries to reason with him. "We'll have to sit here forever if you don't say you are ready." Susan follows her parents' lead and starts to color. Sam holds out for about two more minutes before saying, "I'm ready for you to start driving." Diane says, "Thank you very much. I appreciate your cooperation."

About thirty minutes later another fight starts. Diane starts to pull over to the side of the road, but both kids cry out in unison, "We'll stop. We're ready to keep driving." There was no more fighting for the rest of the day, and the Smiths had a great time at the zoo.

> True discipline is one of the most loving things a parent can provide for a child.

What is the difference between the Jones family and the Smith family? Are Jonathan and Jenny really "bad" kids? No, the difference is that the Smiths are helping their children learn cooperation and problem-solving skills while the Joneses are helping their children learn manipulation skills. The difference is that Mr. and Mrs. Smith demonstrate that they say what they mean and mean what they say by using kind and firm follow-through. Mr. and Mrs. Jones do not. Their angry threats have a temporary effect, but the kids will soon be fighting again.

True discipline is one of the most loving things a parent can provide for a child. All children test boundaries, but believe it or not, children only *think* they want you to give in. Children need to know they can trust the adults in their lives to mean what they say, act reasonably and consistently, and provide security and safety. When adults follow through kindly and firmly, children learn trust and belonging.

The Purpose of Discipline

WHAT SORT OF adults do you want your children to grow up to be? Every conversation, every crisis, every act of discipline can contribute to their development as capable, confident people. Remember that warmth and trust, special time, encouragement, communication, and understanding are tools of discipline, too. When these tools and principles are a part of your everyday life, you'll need the other sort far less often. The way you interact with your children and stepchildren will teach them a great deal about respect, responsibility, trust, and dignity.

15

Yours, Mine, and Ours

Dealing with Money, Houses, and Other Real-Life Issues

IT MAY SEEM THAT stepfamilies have their hands full just understanding relationships and deciding on parenting skills. But your family also must deal with other aspects of life in the everyday world. You and your partner must decide where to live and how to divide the available space. You must make clear arrangements with schools, doctors, churches, and child care providers and take care of necessary legal requirements.

Most newlyweds must figure out who will earn the money, how it will be handled, and who will have the right to spend it—and on what. However, couples in a new stepfamily often bring money, houses, cars, and furniture to the relationship. The big question becomes "What is yours, mine, and ours?" Partners also may bring debts, child support, and alimony obligations. Who is going to pay these bills? For most stepfamilies, each of these decisions can become weighted with emotional meaning.

Family Finances

LIKE IT OR NOT, money matters. There's an old joke that the two issues couples are most likely to argue about are sex and money; there's more truth in that saying than you may like to admit. Earning and managing money are stressful issues for almost all American families these days, but stepfamilies usually must think financial matters through more carefully than most. Unfortunately, many couples are uncomfortable discussing money. They may fear that talking about money somehow indicates a lack of love or trust. They may want to feel financially independent but be unable to express that need. They worry about separating his money from her money from their money. And they may not get around to taking a look at their new family's financial situation until it has already become a trouble spot.

Children and adults frequently equate money—who has it, who gets it, and who can spend it—with love and commitment. Moreover, they're not above comparing their share with everyone else's. Take Greta and Michael, for example. Greta has two children, both in high school. The children live with her and Michael, and she receives child support from her ex-husband. Michael's three children live with his ex-wife in another state; he pays child support and a small amount of alimony each month.

Both Greta and Michael work, and their own young son goes to day care each day. Greta earns slightly more than Michael does. Greta's children both have a number of extracurricular activities

Like it or not, money matters.

("Most of them expensive," grumbles Michael), and one will start college next year. The family moved into a new home two years after their marriage, but now Greta and Michael are worried that they won't be able to continue making the payments when Greta's son starts college.

Although Michael and Greta love each other very much, lately they've been arguing a lot about money. Greta resents the alimony Michael pays to his ex-wife; after all, they need that money themselves. Michael believes that Greta and her ex-husband should be responsible for their son's college expenses. Even though Greta thinks Michael's opinion is logical, she feels hurt that he is unwilling to help support her son, who has lived with them since the beginning of their relationship. The couple also argues frequently about what each should contribute toward the house payment, food and clothing, the utility bills, and their son's child care expenses.

Last night, when Greta suggested that the family take a summer vacation, Michael said flatly, "We can't afford it," without looking up from his newspaper. Greta ran to the bedroom in tears. "How," she wondered, dabbing cold water on her eyes, "could money have become so important?"

Money can be a blessing, a way to create comfort and harmony for your family. Money also can be used as a tool to control and manipulate. Each

FIGURING OUT FINANCES: RESOLVING YOUR DIFFERENCES ABOUT MONEY

Most couples occasionally disagree about money and how it should be managed. Here are some suggestions for resolving difficulties:

1. Talk about it.
2. Take a look ahead.
3. Decide together how to handle money.
4. Jointly determine what is appropriate for the children.
5. Get help when you need it.
6. Consider the legal issues.

family's priorities, circumstances, and needs will be different, but you should keep several things in mind when arranging your family's finances:

1. Talk about it. Discuss money before your marriage, if at all possible! (And it doesn't count if you only talk about it when you are upset.) Choose a time when you are both calm and feeling good. Yes, it can feel awkward to discuss finances; but in the long run both partners will feel more secure when they have a clear understanding of the situation. Be prepared to share information about income, child support and alimony obligations, and outstanding debts. It will help if you take notes so that you can see what it looks like in black and white.

> Children and adults frequently equate money—who has it, who gets it, and who can spend it—with love and commitment.

2. Take a look ahead. What does your new family face in the future? Are there upcoming college, dental, orthodontic, or medical expenses? Who will be responsible? What provisions have been made for investment and retirement? Is medical insurance available? Whose employer offers the best plan? Who will insure whose children? To whom (and to whose children) will any assets be left if one or the other spouse dies?

3. Decide together how to handle money. Once you have all the information in black and white, plan together on what sacrifices might be necessary to plan for the future. You might play a game of "give and take" so that you both realize that each is giving in some areas so the family can take in other areas. Keep talking and brainstorming until you can reach agreements regarding the handling of your money and other assets.

There are two basic approaches: the common account and separate accounts. Some couples pool their resources and income and distribute funds as needed. This approach requires a fairly high level of trust and communication. Some couples find it more convenient to maintain separate accounts and have each partner pay his or her own children's expenses from his or her account, with both making contributions to joint expenses such as housing.

Either approach can work well, as long as both partners agree and can talk about problems calmly. Be sure you discuss how child support money will be used and who will be responsible for expenses such as child care, medical and dental, activities, travel, education (particularly college), and clothing. You might also want to take time to look at credit cards and how each partner feels about their use (and abuse). Remember, prevention is the easiest way to solve a problem.

4. Jointly determine what is appropriate for the children. Children learn to handle money by having some to handle, but parents often don't agree on exactly how this should happen. Some families allow children to make their own decisions about spending and saving, trusting that they will learn from the results of their choices, while others require children to save a certain percentage of whatever money they receive. You will want to agree on whether your children will receive an allowance, how much each child should receive, and who will provide it. Allowances are another topic well suited for discussion at a family meeting.

5. Get help when you need it. Forming a stepfamily these days is a great deal like forming a business partnership; there are many details to consider. You may save time and money in the long run by having a financial planner, accountant, or credit counselor help you decide on a workable approach to managing your money. Go prepared with past tax returns and copies of your divorce decrees, which often list important details such as who gets the dependent deduction for your children. Consulting an expert may help you ensure that your family prospers in the years ahead.

6. Consider the legal issues. Laws vary widely from state to state, but in most states stepfamily relationships are not legally recognized, and stepchildren do not have an automatic right of inheritance from stepparents. When you remarry, it is probably wise to have a new will drawn up, making clear to whom you want your assets, property, and heirlooms to go.

Save time and money by having a financial planner, accountant, or credit counselor help you decide on a workable approach to managing your money.

It is also wise to explore what will happen should one partner predecease the other. Whose children will inherit? At what age will your children be able to manage whatever inheritance they receive? Should you establish a trust? A conversation with a capable attorney who deals in wills and estates may be a wise step toward a future that feels secure for you and your children.

What About Adoption?

Q: I am contemplating marrying a woman who has a four-year-old boy. Her husband passed away when the boy was two. I want to adopt the boy and have him take my name. I think being a coordinated tribe would be good, especially since his mom and I want to have children of our own someday. She wants her son to retain his father's name as a sort of tribute to him. I have no children of my own, and this is an important moral issue for me. What should I do?

A: As with most things in life, there are both pluses and minuses to what you are considering. It can be easier when all the children in a family have the same name, particularly where school records or legal actions are concerned. Still, as your adopted son grows older he will undoubtedly have questions about his birth dad. This is not a man who abandoned him or, apparently, one who treated him or his mother badly. This boy will want both to learn about his birth father and to have a close connection with the man who is raising him: you.

Your adopted son probably can keep his father's name and still love, honor, and respect you. If he has siblings one day and feels that his different name singles him out, you could change his name at that point. If the decision is your son's, he will never hold it against you. Children have a remarkable ability to love many adults and to keep their roles straight. Be assured that it isn't necessary for your son to carry your last name to respect and appreciate you.

The issue of legally adopting stepchildren is a particularly tricky one for many families. A parent who wants to adopt should ask him- or herself some tough questions. Is this an ego trip, or is it an act that will increase belonging and family connection? What does the child want? Is the child old and mature enough to participate in the decision? Adoption may be an issue that is best left for later in the family's journey together: If adults don't force the issue prematurely, children often request it themselves as family connection and closeness increase.

Although adoption does set up a legal relationship and symbolizes caring and commitment, it is usually not possible unless a birth parent is dead or has given up parental rights, a situation that is often emotionally difficult for children. It is undoubtedly best to consult with an attorney about the legal ramifications of remarriage and adoption.

Looking for Solutions

REMEMBER GRETA AND Michael? After seeking help from a counselor, they learned to discuss money issues with dignity and respect during their couple's meetings. They listed every issue: child support (both received and paid), the alimony obligation, earnings, extracurricular activities, college expenses, the mortgage and other living expenses, and summer vacation. They then dealt with one issue at a time in the following manner.

First, they each took ten minutes to express their feelings on the issue. During Greta's monologue, Michael did not interrupt, nor did Greta speak when it was Michael's turn. To ensure that even their body language could not be interpreted as an interruption, they decided to sit on the couch looking straight ahead while the other took a turn. Both found it interesting that, as they spoke for ten whole minutes without interruption, deep resentments surfaced. However, when all the resentments were verbalized, an amazing thing happened: They began to empathize with the other's point of view.

The second thing they did was brainstorm for solutions to each issue. They decided to make their brainstorm session fun by starting out with wild and crazy ideas like winning the lottery, putting their children to work in sweatshops, or moving to a desert island. After this, practical ideas seemed to flow.

The third step was to choose a solution from their list that felt fair and respectful to both of them. If they couldn't find an amicable solution, they agreed to table that issue until a later date. Occasionally, they decided to include the children in their brainstorming sessions. They had to laugh when the children came up with brilliant ideas that had escaped their own efforts.

Greta and Michael found themselves able to discuss a wealth of practical solutions when they worked together in a spirit of love and respect instead of reacting out of resentment and anger.

Living Arrangements: Where Is Home, and What Should We Do Once We Get There?

Q: I just married a wonderful woman who has two children who are ten and six years of age. Her ex lives in another state, so the kids spend almost all of their time with us. My nine-year-old daughter comes over several weekday afternoons and spends every other weekend with us. We're in the process of building a new house, and everything is disorganized. My daughter complains that she has no place of her own to keep things, and lately her behavior has been deteriorating; she whines and is getting more and more defiant with both me and her stepmother. I have to admit that we've been keeping her bureau and her things in the garage because we're short of space. The other kids are with us more often, so they have the bedrooms. (My daughter sleeps on a futon in her stepsister's room.) Could this arrangement be causing our problems?

A: For just a moment, step outside your logical adult world and step into your daughter's world. What does your home *feel* like to her? How does she feel about herself when she's with you? Children's behavior often is a sort of "code" for the feelings and messages they cannot find words for. Your daughter may be feeling like an outsider, a visitor who isn't important enough to have her own space. She may have decided that defiance and complaining are the most effective tools in her possession for getting noticed.

Building a home is a major project and almost always creates tension and chaos. But if you can find a small space to offer your daughter, she may be able to feel more of a sense of belonging and significance when she is with you. You can also invite her to join family meetings where all of you can explore solutions to your challenging living arrangements together.

"Home Is Where the Heart Is"— and So Much More!

LIKE MONEY, LIVING space often becomes a symbol and may represent far more to family members than just a place to sleep. *Home* is a powerful word, and the homes we build together tell a great deal about who we are. Remarrying adults usually have their own tastes and preferences. Each may own a complete set of furnishings and have definite ideas about where everything should go. Children want their own space, room for their belongings, and a place to study or simply be alone. There's an old saying about having "a place for everything and everything in its place," but in stepfamilies that may be easier said than done!

The conventional wisdom about stepfamilies and houses has always been that it is best to start a new family in a new home, one where no one needs to deal with existing territorial boundaries or lingering memories. Moving together into a new home may resolve some issues (although plenty will still

remain), but it also means making changes that the family may find unacceptable. Moving usually means that children must change schools and leave friends, neighbors, and activities behind. Financial barriers to moving into a new home may also exist.

Like money, living space often becomes a symbol and may represent far more to family members than just a place to sleep.

If you move into the home of one partner, be aware that everyone will have feelings about the situation. Those just arriving may feel like intruders and find it hard to create a feeling of ownership and comfort (not to mention find space for their possessions). Those who were there first may believe they have "squatter's rights" and find it difficult to allow someone else to move into their space or to do things in a different way. More than one adult has been dismayed to discover that a helpful new partner has completely reorganized the kitchen (or closet, or garage), and now he or she can't find a thing! Plan on practicing effective communication skills—and on having lots of couple's and family meetings. And don't rule out the possibility of remodeling or adding on.

Wherever you decide to live, keeping a few points in mind will probably help everyone make a smooth transition:

1. Divide the space as fairly as possible. But remember, fair doesn't necessarily mean equal. Sometimes it's just not possible for each child and each

WHO SLEEPS WHERE? SORTING OUT LIVING ARRANGEMENTS

1. Divide the space as fairly as possible.

2. Create ways for everyone to contribute.

3. Count the costs—financial and otherwise.

adult to have equal shares of the available space. Boys may have to share rooms, for example, while a girl gets her own. Or a child who only visits during the summer may have to share space. Still, be sure you think things through; check in with the children occasionally to discover what they are thinking, feeling, and deciding about their living arrangements and what these arrangements mean. When children are consulted respectfully, they often find solutions with a spirit of cooperation.

2. Create ways for everyone to contribute. If your family is moving into a new home, get everyone involved in decorating, arranging furniture, and moving in. If you're moving into a home previously occupied by one partner, be sensitive to the feelings the "resident" family will have, as well as the feelings of the "newcomers."

One family decided to have "work weekends," during which they worked together to paint, wallpaper, and rearrange furniture to create a new look. Another family rotated pictures, knickknacks, and artwork on a regular basis so that everyone's special possessions could be enjoyed. Yet another family decided together which articles and furnishings to keep and sold the unnecessary items at a garage sale, using the proceeds for a family vacation. Be open to suggestions; remember that you are creating a home—comfortable, secure, and welcoming—for everyone in your new family. It may be wiser to make room for someone's favorite, ratty rocking chair than to insist on a decorator-perfect look.

3. Count the costs—financial and otherwise. Financial costs are only part of the decision families must make about where to live. The emotional costs of the decision are often just as important. You may decide that while moving to a new home is expensive, it matters most to have a fresh, new place to begin life together. Or you may decide that the most important consideration is allowing children to remain in a familiar school with their friends.

We realize that we're beginning to sound like a broken record, but family meetings are a wonderful way to explore everyone's needs and feelings. Although ultimately adults must make the family's major financial decisions, you'll probably have to fight fewer battles when everyone feels heard and understood.

Little Things Mean a Lot

DAN MURPHY LOOKED around the dinner table at the smiling faces and lifted his glass in a toast.

"Here's to us," he said with a smile. "We made it to our third anniversary!" Dan, Kelly, and their four children clinked each other's glasses and then settled in to eat dinner, chatting together merrily.

Kelly looked around the circle. "I remember when things weren't this peaceful," she said. "In fact, I remember dinners when all we did was argue about who got to sit next to whom!"

The children looked at each other sheepishly. Kim, 13, grinned at her mom. "Well, I always got to sit next to you before you guys got married. And I couldn't understand why you'd want to sit next to a *man!*"

Kelly laughed, then said, "We used to fight about all sorts of things. Do you remember?"

Rob, nine, piped up, "You and Dad always argued about who got the remote control."

"Yeah," added 10-year-old Eric, "and we had a big fight about what to eat on Christmas Eve." The family laughed as they remembered that epic battle: Dan's children had always had pizza, while Kelly's family looked forward to prime rib.

"And you and Dan couldn't agree on whether to throw tinsel on the tree or put on one strand at a time," Kim finished.

Kelly, Dan, and their children could laugh at their disagreements as they looked back on them, but during the turbulent times when stepfamilies are learning to live together, even the smallest issue can have dramatic significance. Everything seems to have emotional value, and even the smallest change seems to hurt someone's feelings.

> Although ultimately adults must make the family's major financial decisions, you'll probably have to fight fewer battles when everyone feels heard and understood.

Each member of your family—children, teenagers, and adults—is looking for belonging and significance. Most people attach great meaning to familiar possessions and ways of doing things. Who sits where at the family table, whose pictures hang on the wall, what foods a family eats, and which television shows to watch—all can become subjects of heated debate. When you take a moment to search for the beliefs behind these behaviors and preferences, you often realize that (as with so many issues) listening, understanding, and good problem-solving skills will help resolve disagreements. So, undoubtedly, will the passage of time.

Experts tell us that it takes anywhere from three to seven years for a stepfamily to truly settle in together, routines to become familiar, and people to feel comfortable. (They also tell us that the first year or two can feel pretty chaotic.) We'll look a little later on at ways to create new traditions and to build a new family identity. For the moment, remember that there is simply no substitute for patience. Learn to see squabbles and disagreements over money, food, and other issues for what they often are—ways each person looks for love and belonging. Time, trust, understanding, and respect will usually see you through these difficulties to better times.

16

Sexuality and the Stepfamily

What You Might Like to Ignore but Probably Should Not

ALLISON WAS 16 YEARS old when her mother, Carla, married Tom. Allison knew Tom had a son just about her age, but Grant lived with his mother and Allison had seen him only a few times. When Tom and Carla married, Grant decided to move in with his dad—and life for Allison became very interesting indeed.

Allison was bright, pretty, and popular. She had always received her share of male attention; after all, she was on the drill team and pep squad and had recently been elected student body vice president at her high school. Grant was 17, athletic, and funny. Allison felt shy around him at first, but it's hard to stay aloof from someone you meet on your way to and from the shower in the morning. It didn't take long to realize that Grant, emerging from the bathroom in his boxer shorts, was good-looking and that his eyes followed Allison as she passed him, clad in the long T-shirt she wore to bed.

Carla and Tom were immersed in their own relationship; between work and the hours they spent alone in their bedroom, they failed to notice the growing attraction between Allison and Grant. The two young people avoided each other at school and rarely mentioned one another to their friends. Liking your stepsibling was a little weird, and they were uneasy about letting anyone know how they felt. Instead, they rushed home after school when the house was deserted and spent time listening to music, talking, and, eventually, kissing and touching each other.

Adults remarry, and all too often they assume that because they are now a family, sexual attraction between members is out of the question.

One evening Carla poked her head into Allison's room to remind her about a dental appointment the next day and found Grant sitting next to Allison on the bed. Something in the way they leaned toward each other alarmed Carla.

"What do you two think you're doing!" she almost shouted. "You're brother and sister! Grant, get to your room this instant. And Allison, you're not to have him in here when you're alone!"

The two teens received a stern lecture from their parents, but it was going to take more than a lecture to keep them apart. Grant and Allison believed they were in love and that having sex together was the next step. They made love almost every afternoon. They were careful; their parents noticed only that both teens gradually dropped out of their extracurricular activities. They no longer dated or went out with friends, and their grades began to suffer.

One afternoon Carla returned home unexpectedly in the middle of the afternoon to pick up a report she needed for a presentation at work. She heard muffled voices and sighs from down the hall and, curious, went to investigate. The scene that followed was traumatic and painful for everyone. Tom was called home from work; he and Carla were angry, shocked, and disgusted. Allison and Grant were defensive, ashamed—and very scared. Grant was packed off to his mother's home for the remainder of the school year, while Allison barely managed to pass her classes. She mourned her lost love, refused to go out, and withdrew from her mother, who was by now riddled with guilt and worry. The family would never be quite the same, and they all knew it.

Allison and Grant's story may read like fiction, but similar stories take place in stepfamilies every day. Adults remarry, and all too often they assume that because they are now a family, sexual attraction between members is out of the question. And in many, many families, those adults are proved wrong.

Awareness and an Ounce of Prevention

AWARENESS IS AN important part of family life. Try to avoid parenting as though you have a paper bag on your head. It is important to be aware of the ages and stages of your children and to discuss issues openly. We have talked about getting into your child's world when dealing with misbehavior; effective parenting requires the ability to get into your child's world about developmental issues as well.

Carla and Tom were wearing blinders when they assumed that stepsiblings are the same as birth siblings. It is quite different to grow up as siblings than to be introduced to a stepsibling when hormones are more prevalent than common sense. Even stepsiblings who have known each other since they were toddlers may find their feelings toward each other change when they become teenagers. They know that they aren't "real" brother and sister, related by blood.

Discuss sexual issues openly during a family meeting with teenagers. Yes, they (and probably you) will be embarrassed. However, momentary embarrassment may be worthwhile if you can prevent the kind of humiliation and pain experienced by Carla, Tom, Allison, and Grant. Let your teenagers know that you understand hormones and sexual attraction. Get them involved in a discussion about how all of you can handle these situations in your family so that common sense takes precedence over hormones. While you're at it, talk about your

> It is quite different to grow up as siblings than to be introduced to a stepsibling when hormones are more prevalent than common sense.

couple relationship (in gentle, age-appropriate ways, of course) so everyone can explore their feelings, deal with their awkwardness, and learn how to be respectful as they get used to honeymooning parents and stepparents.

Honeymooning with an Audience

COUPLES MARRYING FOR the first time usually have the luxury of privacy. They can get to know each other intimately, express their affection openly, and savor the joys of being together. Newlywed couples with children, however, find themselves in a very different situation. A curious audience is watching their every move, and even young children can be surprisingly aware of the physical attraction between their parents. In many stepfamilies, sexual energy

and tension seem to pervade the atmosphere; young people are usually aware and curious but lack the skills to discuss this sensitive subject calmly.

One stepmother told of hearing her seven-year-old daughter, Kristi, whispering with a friend.

"They sleep in the same room," Kristi said, "but I'm pretty sure they don't do anything."

"I bet they do," her friend replied.

"Eeeeww," Kristi groaned, and both girls dissolved into giggles.

> Even young children can be surprisingly aware of the physical attraction between their parents.

Some couples are afraid to let their children see physical contact and affection between them, but interestingly enough, recent studies show that children tend to have healthier relationships as adults when they witness healthy, appropriate affection between their parents. Notice, however, the word *appropriate.* Some aspects of adult relationships simply belong behind closed doors.

It is unwise to share details of your intimate relationship with children, regardless of their age. Even when they're curious, most children are uncomfortable knowing (or seeing) too much. Each family's feelings will be different; but as a general rule, hugging and affectionate touching are fine—in fact, children often are pleased and reassured by their parents' happiness—but sexual contact should happen in private.

Remember, even when your children like and respect your new partner, their own sense of divided loyalties may make their reactions to your romance more complicated than you realize. Practicing patience and discretion is almost always the best way to proceed.

Sexuality in the Stepfamily

STEPFAMILIES BRING TOGETHER adults and children who are not related by blood. Because the atmosphere in a stepfamily (especially a new one) can contain a lot of sexual energy, families eventually have to decide how they will handle sexuality—especially if teenagers are part of the scene.

For better or worse, sex is part of our everyday culture. Sex is used to sell everything from beer to automobiles; it appears on prime-time television and in movies. Even young children these days are considerably more sophisticated about sex and adult relationships than they used to be, while many adolescents have become sexually active. You may deplore the current situation and moan about the loss of innocence and moral standards; however, since parents are the primary teachers, you also need to give some thought to what you want your young people to learn.

Sexuality is a normal, healthy part of adult relationships, and certainly nothing is wrong with enjoying the company of someone you love. Remember, though, that children will form their ideas about what is right and wrong, appropriate and in-

> Children tend to have healthier relationships as adults when they witness healthy, appropriate affection between their parents. Notice, however, the word *appropriate*.

appropriate, by watching you. What they observe in your new marriage may be very different from what they witnessed in their original family, and it may be wise to check their perceptions and feelings occasionally. Even when they like their new stepparent, children may be-lieve that kissing, hand holding, and other forms of physical intimacy are somehow disloyal to their other parent.

Children may also suffer from occasional pangs of jealousy and see their new stepparent as "competition" for their birth parent's attention and affection. Many new couples have had the somewhat unsettling experience of sitting on the sofa watching a movie and having a child wedge him- or herself between them in a wordless demand for belonging. If you can combine understanding with kind, firm boundaries, the situation will almost always resolve itself in time.

Sexual attraction doesn't necessarily happen only between young people. Sometimes teens (and even preteens) are intrigued by the presence of a new adult of the opposite sex in their home and may explore the boundaries of this new relationship in ways that make everyone uncomfortable. One stepfather came to his parenting group for help with his 15-year-old stepdaughter.

> Children may believe that kissing, hand holding, and other forms of physical intimacy are somehow disloyal to their other parent.

"I always felt comfortable with her," he said, "until her mom and I moved in together. Now she's taken to walking around the house in her underwear or her nightgown, parading around in front of me in a way I find hard to ignore. Last night she came out in a very skimpy nightie and sat in my lap. Her mother was horrified; I was totally embarrassed and didn't know what to do."

Other stepparents have reported similar experiences with stepchildren who seem to be looking for attention, while some stepparents admit feeling attracted to their adolescent stepchildren. Guilt, shame, and embarrassment do little to solve the problem. Honest, open communication, reflective listen-

DEALING WITH SEXUAL ISSUES IN YOUR STEPFAMILY

1. Face the issue squarely.
2. Be sensitive about touching.
3. Be firm about boundaries with children.
4. Consider discussing comfort zones so everyone feels respected and safe.
5. If necessary, consider getting help from a professional.

ing, sensitivity, and patience can help you work through these issues together.

Living together as a stepfamily is a process, and adjusting to the presence of new family members who may be attractive (or overly curious) is part of that process. Successful stepfamilies remember that comfort and peace depend on having dignity and mutual respect. Talking through this aspect of being a family can help everyone if it is handled calmly and with sensitivity. Here are some suggestions:

> Successful step-families remember that comfort and peace depend on having dignity and mutual respect.

1. Face the issue squarely. If you and your partner recognize that your children are of an age when they might be curious or even attracted to one another (or could feel an attraction to one of you), don't ignore the situation in hopes it will go away. Remember your effective communication skills; let children know they can ask you questions and that you can discuss sexuality with them calmly. Pay attention to what you notice, but don't be suspicious or overly concerned—you might create the very thing you fear.

2. Be sensitive about touching. Touch is a wonderful gift; there are times when nothing says quite as much as a hug! Still, adults must be cautious about when and where they touch children, especially teens and preteens. Hugs and kisses that happen before children (or adults, for that matter) are ready for them feel awkward and uncomfortable. Even tickling can create problems if it is carried to extremes.

It may be wise to let children determine how and when they will be touched. Some stepparents tell children, "I feel like giving you a hug. Is that okay with you?" Others wait and let children initiate physical contact, simply letting them know they are open to the idea. Even young children should be taught that they control their bodies and have the right to say no to touch they find uncomfortable. Some families make an agreement that when *any*one says, "Please stop!" about touching, that request must be honored. Children also should know that secrets about touching are not okay and that they can always tell a parent when they're having a problem.

3. Be firm about boundaries with children. If children touch you inappropriately or act in ways that make you uncomfortable, let them know kindly but firmly that what they are doing is not okay with you. Remember that

> Children also should know that secrets about touching are not okay and that they can always tell a parent when they're having a problem.

touching that happens in the wrong way or at the wrong time usually creates distance rather than closeness and trust. In the long run, you will probably do your family a favor by asking that boundaries be respected. It isn't necessary to blame, shame, or humiliate; simply let children know that you appreciate their affection but would prefer they show it in different ways. Be gentle but specific about what is okay with you.

4. Consider discussing comfort zones so everyone feels respected and safe. You may want to talk with your family about sexuality and respect. Obviously, how you handle this will depend on the ages of your children, but it may be wise to agree on such things as entering bedrooms, bathroom behavior, nudity, and other sensitive topics. Partners sometimes disagree about what is acceptable; one may be quite comfortable with scanty attire while the other prefers bathrobes.

Have a couple's meeting to explore your own preferences and beliefs; it may then be appropriate to have a family meeting to brainstorm comfort zones with children. Remember, every member of the family has the right to feel respected and to ask for what he or she needs. Sensitivity now may save you problems later on.

5. If necessary, consider getting help from a professional. Sometimes sexual behavior is just too difficult to discuss calmly in the family. At such times, a competent counselor or pastor may be helpful. Seeking help is not an admission of failure; sometimes it's the wisest and most loving thing parents can do. You want your children to grow up to be healthy, loving adults who can enjoy healthy, loving relationships; you also want the freedom to enjoy your relationship with your partner. Getting help may be a good investment in your future together.

> Seeking help is not an admission of failure; sometimes it's the wisest and most loving thing parents can do.

Physical closeness and affection can be among the best parts of being a family—when they happen in the right way. It's normal to feel a little uncomfortable with new family members, especially at the beginning. Remember that respect and sensitivity now will pave the way for warmth and closeness as you grow together.

17

Tying It All Together

Building a New Family Identity

W HAT DO YOU remember about the family in which you grew up? Most adults carry with them a hodgepodge of recollections—some pleasant, some painful. But among the memories most people cherish are the times they felt "like a family": during the rituals, traditions, and celebrations that families develop over time, the moments of laughter and playfulness. Most people can remember special foods at the holiday table or a particular plate the birthday child ate from; they remember traditions lovingly passed from generation to generation. If they don't have such things to remember, they often wish they did.

When death, divorce, or separation divides a family, its traditions sometimes fade away. Perhaps they are no longer appropriate or bring back painful memories. When a stepfamily forms, its members may find that they have separate histories and traditions, little of which is shared. We've explored the hectic world that stepfamilies inhabit; we've looked at conflicts and problems and ways of resolving them. Now it is time to look at the characteristics that make a family more than just a group of people who live together. After all, the rituals and rhythms of life, together with the relationships you build with those around you, are what give life its meaning.

Becoming "We" Through Traditions and Celebrations

WE'VE MENTIONED BEFORE that it can take anywhere from three to seven years for a stepfamily to settle down, to feel comfortable and natural. If this has already happened for you, congratulations! If not, relax and recognize that you can do a number of things to build a new identity as a family.

> Among the memories most people cherish are the times they felt "like a family": during the rituals, traditions, and celebrations developed over time, the moments of laughter and playfulness.

Human beings are amazing creations. Each of us is unique; each of us possesses talents, gifts, and qualities that make us special. For that reason, the families we make are unique as well. Differences can sometimes be perceived as things that separate us from each other, but consider for a moment that not one other family on earth is like yours. Recognizing—and learning to celebrate—the things that make you different can be a giant step on the journey toward closeness and trust.

Some day soon, sit down with your partner and your children. Take a large sheet of paper and start thinking, talking, and writing down the qualities, activities, and ideas that make you who you are. Each person in your family—"step" or birth—has interests and talents. What are they? Is there a special atmosphere or energy in your home that others no-

BECOMING "WE": CREATING UNITY IN YOUR STEPFAMILY

Becoming a family in which each person feels comfortable takes time, but there are some ways you can encourage the process:

1. Create a family portrait gallery.

2. Celebrate your differences and uniqueness.

3. Make a family quilt.

4. Create nonverbal signals or sign language unique to your family.

5. Reach out to others.

Your family meetings are a wonderful place to brainstorm other ideas for drawing you together as a family.

tice? Do you have a funny or encouraging motto or slogan? Do you have pets? Favorite foods?

Write everything down. Use colorful markers, and illustrate your design with pictures clipped from magazines. You may want to let each person have his or her own space on the sheet to draw a personal design. Leave the sheet out for a while; add to it at family meetings. Then post your "family portrait" in a prominent place. Discovering the ways your family members are both different and the same will help build a sense of unity and appreciation, and it may help you discover that your family's differences are among its greatest assets.

Your new family can build a sense of identity and unity in many ways. Remember that real closeness takes time, but you can certainly set the stage. Here are some suggestions:

1. Create a family portrait gallery. Dedicate one wall in your den or hallway to family pictures. Begin with grandparents and baby pictures of each adult. Add pictures of the couple, perhaps including wedding photos. Surround the couple's pictures with photos of each child, whether they live with you full time or only visit. You may want to allow children to select pictures of themselves that have particular meaning or that symbolize something important to each child. Be sure you include photos of all of you together, perhaps enjoying an activity or a shared vacation. A picture wall may be a symbolic gesture, but it will encourage the feeling that you are a family.

2. Celebrate your differences and uniqueness. Your stepfamily may incorporate different ethnic backgrounds, cultural heritages, or races. Set aside some family meetings for learning about each other. Encourage the members of your family to educate each other about their different backgrounds, histories, and traditions. You may want to prepare special foods, tell stories, play music, or share information about your history and cultural traditions. Learning together can be an enjoyable and effective way to create harmony and understanding.

3. Make a family quilt. Give each member of the family a square of fabric to decorate with embroidery, appliqué, glitter pens, or fabric markers. When each person has completed his or her design, join the squares together to make a family quilt. You may choose to make a border from favorite colors or patterns, attach a backing, and either quilt or tie it. While experience with a sewing machine may help, even the inexperienced can produce a bright wall hanging or blanket under which to cuddle together while reading or watching television.

4. Create nonverbal signals or sign language unique to your family. When Brenda and Martin learned that the baby girl they had together had speech and developmental delays, they were devastated and worried about the effect a "special" child who needed extra time and attention might have on the older children each had brought to their new marriage. As little Bethany grew, however, her speech therapist began teaching her sign language, and the older children began to pick it up themselves. Bethany eventually learned to speak quite clearly, but the family continued to use sign language as a way to communicate. Words, they found, sometimes got in the way, while the gestures of sign language became their family's special language—something they all shared that made them feel connected to one another.

You might use a family meeting to develop special ways to communicate things you frequently say in your family. First decide on messages that you find yourself saying over and over, such as "I love you." You might decide on a hand over the heart to convey this message. The referee's signal for time-out might be your family's signal for "Let's take a time-out to calm down until we can discuss this respectfully." Wide arms, hulking shoulders, and wiggling fingers might be the signal for "Do it now or the impatient monster will get you." A cheek resting on praying hands might be the signal for bedtime. Your family will be able to think of many more.

> Learning to celebrate the things that make you different can be a giant step on the journey toward closeness and trust.

It is often said that a picture is worth a thousand words. The humor of nonverbal signals (especially when they have been agreed on in advance) often breaks the tension of a situation that has become too negative. Also, a nonverbal signal is usually more inviting than lectures in a tone of voice that conveys anger or disgust.

5. Reach out to others. Doing something as a family that helps others or improves your community can draw you together in a powerful way. Volunteer for a park or trail cleanup, or "adopt" a less privileged family at the holidays or even year-round. Hold a neighborhood barbecue or a church softball game; visit the elderly or read to hospitalized children. Several organizations provide opportunities for families to adopt a child in another country for as little as $30 a month. What a great way for the whole family to make a contribution to someone in need, especially when the results are shared during your family meetings. Writing letters and sending pictures to your adopted child will have the added benefit of drawing you together as a family. What have you noticed in your own corner of the world that could use some energy? Brainstorm ways to make a contribution at a family meeting.

Remember, becoming a family doesn't mean becoming the same. Recognize and celebrate the unique and valuable contributions each person brings to your stepfamily. The family you create together will be all the richer.

Handling the Holidays

HOLIDAYS CAN BE stressful times for most families, but for families complicated by death, divorce, or remarriage, holidays can be downright crazy. Each partner and set of children may have different expectations and different traditions. There may be several sets of grandparents and extended families to satisfy, some of whom may or may not like the others. Schedules may be complicated, with children coming and going. There may be more people—and less money.

The rituals and traditions that surround special days and celebrations are meant to add joy and meaning to life. If you find that you dread special days and feel more anxiety than joy, it's time to take a closer look at what holidays mean to your family. Spend some time with your partner and children exploring what matters most to each of you about the holidays. Which parts of your old traditions do you cherish and want to keep? Which parts no longer work? What new ideas do you have that will make holidays special for the family you are now?

> No one has perfect holidays, despite the glowing television specials and magazine stories. Decide what works for you, then relax.

Ask your family what is most important to each of them, then develop your family celebrations around those ideas. You may want to invite one partner and his or her children to prepare dinner on Christmas Eve, for instance, while the other partner takes responsibility for Christmas Day. Or you may invite each family member to contribute or cook one item for a family feast. If you have different religious traditions, what are some ways you can combine your celebrations so that everyone feels included?

If both partners have children, with visitation schedules to consider, you may want to consider arranging schedules so that you alternate holidays when all the children are present with holidays when you're alone and able to travel or just enjoy some time together. As much as possible, adjust your expectations to fit your situation. No one has perfect holidays, despite the glowing television specials and magazine stories. Decide what works for you, then relax. Let holidays and celebrations be opportunities to learn more about each other, rather than times to be right or wrong.

Remember, too, that there is nothing magical about the calendar. If a child will be with his or her other parent on Thanksgiving, a birthday, or another special occasion, hold your own celebration on a day when you can be together. Telephone calls, faxes, and funny gifts can be wonderful ways to make a child who lives far away feel special and remembered. Details and dates are less important than building a sense of belonging, of closeness and warmth.

> Ask family members what is most important to each of them, then develop your family celebrations around those ideas.

Be patient; it may take a little experimenting to discover traditions that truly work, but it is worth the effort. Rituals and traditions are not only fun—they draw us together and they heal us. Your stepfamily will grow stronger as you live, work, and celebrate together.

Laughter and Play as a Way to Build Connection

SIX-YEAR-OLD DAVY definitely did not want to go to bed. He had asked for three glasses of water and two bedtime stories and had made several trips to the bathroom. When Gail, his mom, came into the bedroom this time, she was ready for battle.

"That's quite enough, young man," she said sternly. "We have work in the morning, and you have kindergarten. It's time for bed. Now, under the covers—right this minute!"

Davy furrowed his small brow and folded his arms. And then, with all the defiance of a frustrated little boy, he stuck out his tongue at his mother.

Gail was tired and ready for bed herself, but something in the expression on her son's small face amused her. Without stopping to think, she stuck her own tongue out and followed that by grabbing Davy's pillow and giving him a gentle swat on the seat of his pajamas.

Davy was delighted. In two seconds he had his stepbrother's pillow and was returning fire. Gail giggled, then shrieked as a flying pillow whacked her on the ear. Turning around she saw her 12-year-old stepdaughter Abby, another pillow in her hand, and running steps in the hall told her that nine-year-old Tommy was on his way. A full-fledged pillow fight broke out, and it was not long before Steve, Gail's new husband, joined the battle.

> Remember that laughter works best when it's *with* each other rather than *at* each other.

For a while it was grown-ups against the children; then Steve and his children took on Davy and Gail. After that, it was everyone for him- or herself, and pillows flew wildly until the exhausted combatants collapsed in a sweaty, laughing heap. Gail poured cold glasses of milk for everyone, and Davy drew more laughter when he announced solemnly, "It's way past my bedtime. I need to go to sleep."

Will a pillow fight solve every behavior problem? Of course not. But there's no doubt that humor and laughter make life together far more enjoyable. We've explored play as a way to get into a child's world and understand how he thinks and feels, but shared laughter is also an effective way to build a sense of closeness and connection in your stepfamily.

What might happen if a snowball war broke out in your front yard? Or if you played a game of hide-and-seek with the lights out? How many silly knock-knock jokes do the members of your family know? Try having a kite-flying contest or sharing favorite cartoons as part of a family meeting.

Remember that laughter works best when it's *with* each other rather than *at* each other. Nicknames and teasing should come from respect and affection; ridicule is not helpful or healing. Humor and laughter can carry us through even the toughest of times and can help create a family atmosphere where people want to come in and stay awhile.

A Word About You

ONE PART OF the stepfamily that has not yet received much attention so far is you. Yes, you—the person with this book in your hands. We've said more than once that parenting is an important, demanding job—one that requires thoughtfulness, patience, energy, and commitment. It's difficult to do the sort of job you want to when you are discouraged, stressed, or overwhelmed, which can easily happen when you are creating a new family.

Imagine for a moment that you are holding a beautiful crystal pitcher. The pitcher is filled with water, which represents your time, attention, and emotional energy. Throughout the day your partner, your children, your coworkers, and your friends come to you needing your attention. Each time, you pour water from your pitcher—a little bit here, a drop there, a big splash over there. By the end of the day, the pitcher is nearly empty, and at the moment when your water is completely gone, a crisis happens. Your children need you; your partner has an emergency. You reach for your pitcher and realize that it is empty and you can't remember the last time you filled it. Where will you find the energy to deal with what you face?

No one does his or her best work when drained and empty. Taking care of yourself—"filling your pitcher"—is among the most important tasks in creating a healthy stepfamily. Nurturing yourself isn't selfishness; it is wisdom. Building a strong marriage and a strong family is never easy, but it becomes significantly less difficult when each individual in it is healthy. Here are a few suggestions for strengthening and refreshing yourself. While these suggestions

FILLING THE PITCHER: TAKING CARE OF YOURSELF

There are three primary ways of sustaining your own physical and emotional health:

1. Nurture your body.

2. Cultivate your mind.

3. Feed your spirit.

are not new, they are worth repeating; integrating this advice into your daily life can make a significant difference in the way your family feels to each person in it.

1. Nurture your body. Yes, it matters. Loving parents often scrutinize their children's sleep and eating habits and neglect their own. Doctors and therapists can tell you that there is a strong tie between the mind and the body. You will feel far more energetic and alert (and will be more likely to have the courage and motivation it takes to make changes in your family) when you pay attention to what you eat and drink and get adequate sleep.

Exercise, too, is vital; you will sleep better and have more energy when you exercise regularly, and exercise is a natural mood elevator; in fact, research tell us that regular exercise is one of the most effective antidepressants available. You need not dress in Spandex and sweat yourself silly in a gym to enjoy the benefits of exercise. A brisk walk can work wonders. You may enjoy golf, tennis, or skiing with your partner; the entire family may discover they love bicycle outings; and yoga and tai chi nurture the spirit as well as the body. If you don't know where to begin, consult your doctor. Whatever you enjoy, do it regularly for a month and see whether you notice a difference in your attitude and energy level!

> Taking care of yourself—"filling your pitcher"—is among the most important tasks in creating a healthy stepfamily.

2. Cultivate your mind. One harried mother of preschoolers tells the story of going to dinner at an elegant restaurant with business associates and, in the midst of a conversation with the person sitting next to her, realizing she was helpfully cutting his meat into bite-size pieces! Parenting is important and enjoyable work, but sometimes everyone needs adult conversation and a bit of intellectual stimulation. Taking care of yourself may mean curling up with a good book, surfing the Internet, taking an occasional class or two, or even doing volunteer work. Remember that learners inherit the Earth; stretching your mind is as healthy as stretching your body.

> Regular exercise—a natural mood elevator—will help you sleep better and will give you more energy.

One young mother was told by a wise counselor, "If you take one class a semester, you could have a college degree by the time your children are grown." Eleven years and five children later, she had a college degree in child development and family relations. Getting out of the house one night a week increased her enjoyment of her husband and children when she was with them. The children all attended her graduation wearing PMT (Putting Mom Through) buttons on their chests.

3. Feed your spirit. Most folks recognize stress when they have it, but they often have difficulty knowing what to do with it. You have probably noticed that living together as a stepfamily can be stressful at times and that stress can get in the way of even the most loving relationships. How you deal with your

> Your children are more likely to learn respect for self and others when you demonstrate self-respect in your own daily life.

feelings—and, just as important, how you continue to grow as a unique person—is crucial.

Taking care of your body and mind will help you feel stronger emotionally. It's also important that you have time to do the things that you most enjoy—whether music, gardening, tinkering with a hot rod, or collecting stamps. Whatever you love, whatever feeds you spiritually, whatever nurtures the person you truly are, you should do regularly. It is not only important to respect others; it's important to respect yourself. In fact, your children are more likely to learn respect for self and others when you demonstrate self-respect in your own daily life. Providing undue attention and special service to others almost always breeds resentment—and feeling grouchy rarely leads anyone to do his or her best work. Remember that you, too, are a valuable and important person.

"Oh, sure," you may be saying. "Where am I supposed to find time for all this healthy stuff?" Well, that's an excellent question. Nurturing yourself means learning to budget time wisely. It may mean adjusting priorities so that how you spend your time accurately reflects what you truly value. Even if all you can find is a single hour each week to take care of yourself, you—and your family—will be healthier because of that one hour.

Appreciate Each Moment

JESSICA SAT ON the front porch, a cool drink in her hand, breathing in the summer night air and listening to the voices of her family. Jessica and Ted had been married four years, and together they had five children ranging in age from five to sixteen. There had certainly been problems—in fact, a few still lingered. Money was tight with so many active young people around, and time was even harder to find than money. Still, they had had more good times than tough ones, Jessica thought.

The family had just returned from a summer vacation, which they had spent camping in the mountains. It had been quite a trip. They had endured sunburn and mosquito bites. A sudden squall had blown over two tents and doused their campfire in the middle of making s'mores, and little Teddy had managed to throw up on his stepbrother's sleeping bag. There had been squabbling and bickering, and 16-year-old Sarah's ghost stories had been so vivid that the youngest members of the family had been unable to sleep one night. More than once, everyone in the family had wanted to load up the van and head for home. When they finally did, the van had broken down by the side of the road, and they had needed a good Samaritan trucker to give Ted a ride into the nearest town.

Yet now, Jessica heard the children trading vacation stories with more laughter than complaints. Someone threatened good-naturedly to throw up on Teddy's pillow; somewhere Jessica heard Ted's deep voice rumbling over a bedtime story and Sarah helping someone with stubborn pajama buttons.

Suddenly Jessica felt a deep contentment stealing over her. "We sound just like a family," she thought wonderingly, "almost as if we've always been together." She looked out at the twilight and smiled. The past four years hadn't been easy, and

> If we pay attention, if we listen and watch, moments come along when living and growing together feel wonderful.

she knew that more challenges lay ahead. But right now—this moment—was just about perfect. She sat quite still for a moment, savoring the feeling, and then headed inside. Her family would be waiting for good night hugs.

Life in a stepfamily is rarely simple, and will almost certainly never be perfect. But if we pay attention, if we listen and watch, moments do come along when living and growing together feel wonderful. We can share both laughter and tears, hopes and dreams, fears and successes. And we can remember that the only moment we ever really possess is now. The past is gone, and no matter how hard we worry, tomorrow won't come any sooner. This present moment is the only one we can live in, laugh in, and change.

Take a moment to look around you; think of the unique people who make up your stepfamily. See whether you can learn to savor the moments you share. Take time to laugh; be sure the message of love and respect gets through to those you care about. Work toward patience, trust, and faith, and celebrate progress whenever you have the opportunity. Your family will be whatever you have the courage and wisdom to make it.

SELECTED REFERENCES

Berman, Claire. *Making It As a Stepparent: New Roles/New Rules*, updated edition. New York: Harper Perennial, 1986.

Clifton, Donald O., and Paula Nelson. *Soar with Your Strengths.* New York: Dell, 1992.

Doherty, William. Divided Loyalties: The Challenge of Stepfamily Life. *Family Therapy Networker* (May/June 1999): 35.

Dreikurs, Rudolf, with Vicki Soltz. *Children: The Challenge,* revised edition. New York: Plume, 1990.

Einstein, Elizabeth, and Linda Albert. *Strengthening Your Stepfamily.* AGS (1986).

Gottman, John, and Nan Silver. *The Seven Principles for Making Marriage Work.* New York: Crown, 1999.

Larson, J. Understanding Stepfamilies. *American Demographics* 14, no. 360 (1992).

Lott, Lynn, Riki Intner, and Barbara Mendenhall. *Do-It-Yourself Therapy: How to Think, Feel, and Act Like a New Person in Just 8 Weeks.* Franklin Lakes, NJ: Career Press, 1998.

McGoldrick, Monica, and Betty Carter. Forming a Remarried Family. In *The Changing Family Life Cycle: A Framework for Family Therapy*, second edition, edited by Monica McGoldrick and Betty Carter. Needham Heights, MA: Allyn & Bacon, 1989.

Morgan, Kay. Mother, Not-Mother: the Slow Road to Acceptance in a Blended Family. *Family Therapy Networker* (January/February 2000): 57.

Nelsen, Jane. *From Here to Serenity.* Roseville, CA: Prima, 2000.

———. *Positive Time-Out: And Over 50 Ways to Avoid Power Struggles in the Home and the Classroom.* Rocklin, CA: Prima, 1999.

———. *Positive Discipline.* New York: Ballantine, 1996.

Nelsen, Jane, Roslyn Duffy, and Cheryl Erwin. *Positive Discipline: The First Three Years.* Rocklin, CA: Prima, 1998.

———.*Positive Discipline for Preschoolers,* revised second edition. Rocklin, CA: Prima, 1998.

Nelsen, Jane, and Lynn Lott. *Positive Discipline for Teenagers,* revised second edition. Roseville, CA: Prima, 2000.

Pasley, et al. Successful Stepfamily Therapy: Clients' Perspectives. *Journal of Marital and Family Therapy* 22, no. 3 (1996).

Ricci, Isolina. *Mom's House, Dad's House: Making Two Homes for Your Child,* revised edition. New York: Fireside/Simon & Schuster, 1997.

Sanders, G. F. Family Strengths: A National Study. Unpublished thesis, University of Nebraska, Lincoln, Nebraska, 1979.

Schnarch, David. *Passionate Marriage: Keeping Love and Intimacy Alive in Committed Relationships.* New York: Owl Books, 1998.

Stinnett, N., B. Chesser, & J. DeFrain. (eds.) *Building Family Strengths: Blueprints for Action.* Lincoln: Univ. of Nebraska Press, 1979.

Stinnett, N, and J. DeFrain. *Secrets of Strong Families.* New York: Berkley Publishing Group, 1985.

Stinnett, N., B. Knorr, J. DeFrain, and G. Rowe. How Strong Families Cope with Crises. *Family Perspective* 15 (1984): 159-166.

Visher, Emily B., and John S. Visher. *Stepfamilies: Myths and Realities.* New York: Citadel, 1993.

INDEX

ABOUT THE AUTHORS

 **Jane Nelsen** is a popular lecturer and coauthor of the entire POSITIVE DISCIPLINE series. She also wrote *From Here to Serenity: Four Principles for Understanding Who You Really Are.* She has appeared on *Oprah* and *Sally Jesse Raphael* and was the featured parent expert on the "National Parent Quiz," hosted by Ben Vereen. Jane is the mother of seven children and the grandmother of eighteen.

 **Cheryl Erwin** is a licensed marriage and family therapist in private practice, a lecturer and trainer, and the coauthor of four books in the POSITIVE DISCIPLINE series. Cheryl also has a weekly radio broadcast on parenting in the Reno, Nevada, area, where she lives with her husband and 16-year-old son.

 **H. Stephen Glenn** is the creator of Developing Capable People, a course that teaches skills for living and building strong relationships in homes, schools, and organizations. He has coauthored many books, including *Raising Self-Reliant Children in a Self-Indulgent World* and *7 Strategies for Developing Capable Students.* Steve is the father of four children, stepfather of three, and grandfather of ten. He has also been a foster father of several young children.

FOR MORE INFORMATION

THE AUTHORS ARE available for lectures, workshops, and seminars for parents, parent educators, therapists, psychologists, social workers, nurses, counselors, school administrators, teachers, and corporations. (Lectures can be tailored to fit your needs.)

Workshops include:

Positive Discipline in the Classroom (a two-day workshop or a one-day inservice)
Teaching Parenting the Positive Discipline Way (a two-day workshop)
Empowering Teens and Yourself in the Process
Developing Capable People (three-day leadership training)

Workshops, seminars, and facilitator training are scheduled throughout the United States each year. To find a location near you or to bring a workshop to your area, contact:

Jane Nelsen
Positive Discipline Associates
4984 Arboleda Drive
Fair Oaks, CA 95628
1-800-456-7770

Cheryl Erwin
835 N. Rock Boulevard
Sparks, NV 89431
1-775-355-7722
ErwinCL@aol.com

H. Stephen Glenn
Capabilities, Inc.
1-800-222-1494

View www.positivediscipline.com for featured articles, answers to parent and teacher questions, and workshop and research information.

ORDER FORM

To: Empowering People, P.O. Box 1926, Orem, UT 84059
Phone: 1-800-456-7770 (credit card orders only)
Fax: 801-762-0022
Web Site: www.positivediscipline.com for discount prices

BOOKS	Price	Quantity	Amount
Positive Discipline for Your Stepfamily, by Nelsen, Erwin, & Glenn	$16.00	_____	_____
Positive Discipline for Single Parents, by Nelsen, Erwin, & Delzer	$16.00	_____	_____
Positive Discipline in the Classroom, by Nelsen, Lott, & Glenn	$16.95	_____	_____
Positive Discipline: A Teacher's A–Z Guide, by Nelsen, Duffy, Escobar, Ortolano, & Owen-Sohocki	$14.95	_____	_____
Positive Discipline for Preschoolers, by Nelsen, Erwin, & Duffy	$16.00	_____	_____
Positive Discipline: The First Three Years, by Nelsen, Erwin, & Duffy	$16.00	_____	_____
Positive Discipline, by Nelsen	$12.00	_____	_____
Positive Discipline A–Z, by Nelsen, Lott, & Glenn	$16.00	_____	_____
Positive Discipline for Teenagers, by Nelsen & Lott	$16.95	_____	_____
Positive Discipline for Parenting in Recovery, by Nelsen, Intner, & Lott	$12.95	_____	_____
Raising Self-Reliant Children in a Self-Indulgent World, by Glenn & Nelsen	$12.95	_____	_____
Positive Time-Out: And 50 Other Ways to Avoid Power Struggles, Nelsen	$12.00	_____	_____
From Here to Serenity, by Nelsen	$14.00	_____	_____

MANUALS			
Teaching Parenting the Positive Discipline Way, by Lott & Nelsen	$49.95	_____	_____
Positive Discipline in the Classroom, by Nelsen & Lott	$49.95	_____	_____

TAPES AND VIDEOS			
Positive Discipline audiotape	$10.00	_____	_____
Positive Discipline videotape	$49.95	_____	_____
Building Healthy Self-Esteem Through Positive Discipline audiotape	$10.00	_____	_____

SUBTOTAL _____

Sales tax: UT add 6.25%; CA add 7.25% _____

Shipping & handling: $3.00 plus $0.50 each item _____

(Prices subject to change without notice.)   **TOTAL** _____

METHOD OF PAYMENT (check one):
_____ Check made payable to Empowering People Books, Tapes, & Videos
_____ MasterCard, Visa, Discover Card, American Express

Card # _____ Expiration _____ /_____
Ship to _____
Address _____
City/State/Zip _____
Daytime phone (_____)_____

Raise Your Teenager with Positive Discipline

Everyone knows adolescence opens up vast new interests, problems, and potential in children. *Positive Discipline for Teenagers, Revised 2nd Edition,* shows you how to avoid a cycle of guilt and blame and begin working toward greater understanding and communication with your adolescent. Inside, you'll learn:

- **How to win cooperation without threatening**
- **How to see the world through a teen's eyes**
- **How you and your teen can grow and change together**
- **And more!**

ISBN 0-7615-2181-X / Paperback / 368 pages
U.S. $16.95 / Can. $25.00

FEB 2 3 2001

To order, call (800) 632-8676 ext. 4444 or visit us online at www.primalifestyles.com